W9-BMS-200

the LIFE OF CHRIST

Publisher
Richard Fraiman

General Manager
Steven Sandonato

Executive Director, Marketing Services
Carol Pittard

Director, Retail & Special Sales
Tom Mifsud

Director, New Product Development
Peter Harper

Assistant Director, Brand Marketing
Laura Adam

Associate Counsel
Helen Wan

Book Production Manager
Jonathan Polsky

Design & Prepress Manager
Anne-Michelle Gallero

Marketing Manager
Alexandra Bliss

General Editor
Christopher D. Hudson

Senior Editor
Kelly Knauer

Managing Editor
Carol Smith

Consulting Editors from the American Bible Society's Nida Institute for Biblical Scholarship:
Barbara Bernstengel
Robert Hodgson, Ph.D.
With special thanks to the American Bible Society's Committee on Translation and Scholarship

Contributing Writers
Anita Palmer
Gordon Lawrence
Mia Littlejohn
Carol Smith
Randy Southern
Jessica Thomas

Design and Production
Mark Wainwright
Symbology Creative

Special Thanks:
Bozena Bannett
Glenn Buonocore
Robert Marasco
Suzanne Janso
Brooke Reger
Mary Sarro-Waite
Ilene Schreider
Adriana Tierno
Alex Voznesenskiy

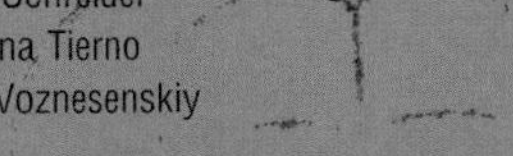

Time Inc.
1271 Avenue of the Americas
New York, New York 10020

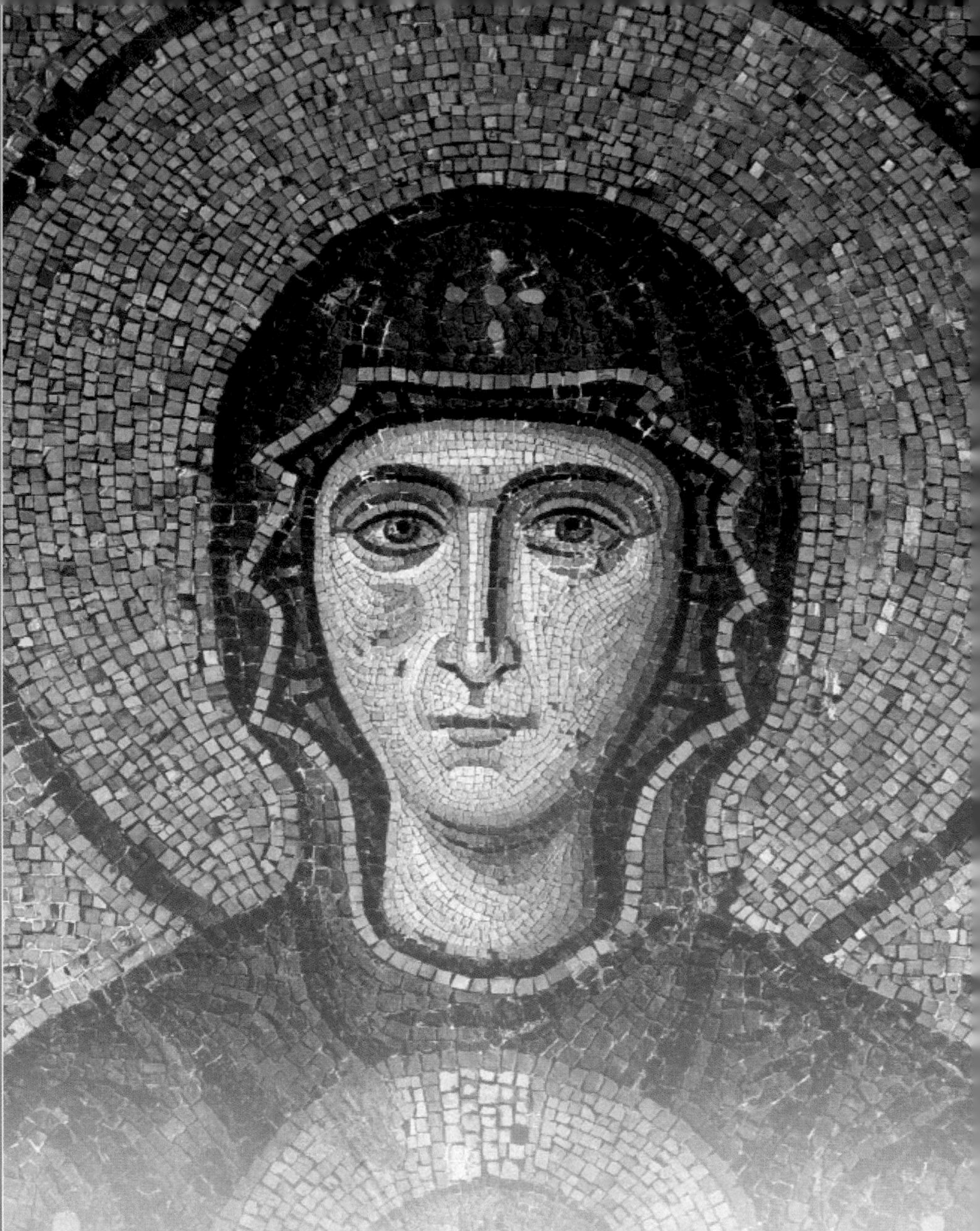

ISBN 13: 978-1-60320-005-9
ISBN 10: 1-60320-005-3
Library of Congress #: 2007908296

We welcome your comments and suggestions about *The Life of Christ*. Please write to us at:
The Life of Christ
Attention: Book Editors
PO Box 11016
Des Moines, IA 50336-1016

If you would like to order any of our hardcover Collector's Edition books, please call us at 1-800-327-6388. (Monday through Friday, 7:00 a.m.–8:00 p.m. or Saturday, 7:00 a.m.– 6:00 p.m. Central Time).

the LIFE OF CHRIST

TABLE OF CONTENTS

the LIFE OF CHRIST

PREFACE

The first-century life and ministry of Jesus of Nazareth is described in the Gospels, the four books that open the New Testament portion of the Bible.

Through his identity, his works, his miracles, and his grass-roots following, Jesus lived out a specific mission—to sacrifice his life so that humanity could connect with God in a new way, unhindered by sin and the brokenness that results from it. He chose a small group in which to invest this mission and ministry and sent them out to continue his work.

Since that time, Jesus' followers have continued to read and re-read the accounts of Jesus and to apply his teachings to their own lives. While there are many variations in how these followers demonstrate and practice their faith, Jesus' story is essential.

To examine the life of Jesus, exploring the new life offered through his death and resurrection, is to learn about the kingdom of heaven in the here and now. It is to explore what it means to be a child of God, to live abundantly, to receive forgiveness, and to find redemption and hope.

IN THE BEGINNING WAS THE ONE WHO IS CALLED THE WORD. THE WORD WAS WITH GOD AND WAS TRULY GOD. FROM THE VERY BEGINNING THE WORD WAS WITH GOD.

AND WITH THIS WORD, GOD CREATED ALL THINGS. NOTHING WAS MADE WITHOUT THE WORD. EVERYTHING THAT WAS CREATED RECEIVED ITS LIFE FROM HIM, AND HIS LIFE GAVE LIGHT TO EVERYONE. THE LIGHT KEEPS SHINING IN THE DARK, AND DARKNESS HAS NEVER PUT IT OUT. GOD SENT A MAN NAMED JOHN, WHO CAME TO TELL ABOUT THE LIGHT AND TO LEAD ALL PEOPLE TO HAVE FAITH. JOHN WASN'T THIS LIGHT. HE CAME ONLY TO TELL ABOUT THE LIGHT.

THE TRUE LIGHT THAT SHINES ON EVERYONE WAS COMING INTO THE WORLD. THE WORD WAS IN THE WORLD, BUT NO ONE KNEW HIM, THOUGH GOD HAD MADE THE WORLD WITH HIS WORD. HE CAME INTO HIS OWN WORLD, BUT HIS OWN NATION DID NOT WELCOME HIM. YET SOME PEOPLE ACCEPTED HIM AND PUT THEIR FAITH IN HIM. SO HE GAVE THEM THE RIGHT TO BE THE CHILDREN OF GOD. THEY WERE NOT GOD'S CHILDREN BY NATURE OR BECAUSE OF ANY HUMAN DESIRES. GOD HIMSELF WAS THE ONE WHO MADE THEM HIS CHILDREN.

THE WORD BECAME A HUMAN BEING AND LIVED HERE WITH US. WE SAW HIS TRUE GLORY, THE GLORY OF THE ONLY SON OF THE FATHER. FROM HIM THE COMPLETE GIFTS OF UNDESERVED GRACE AND TRUTH HAVE COME DOWN TO US.

JOHN 1:1-14

The Historical Context *of the* Life of Christ

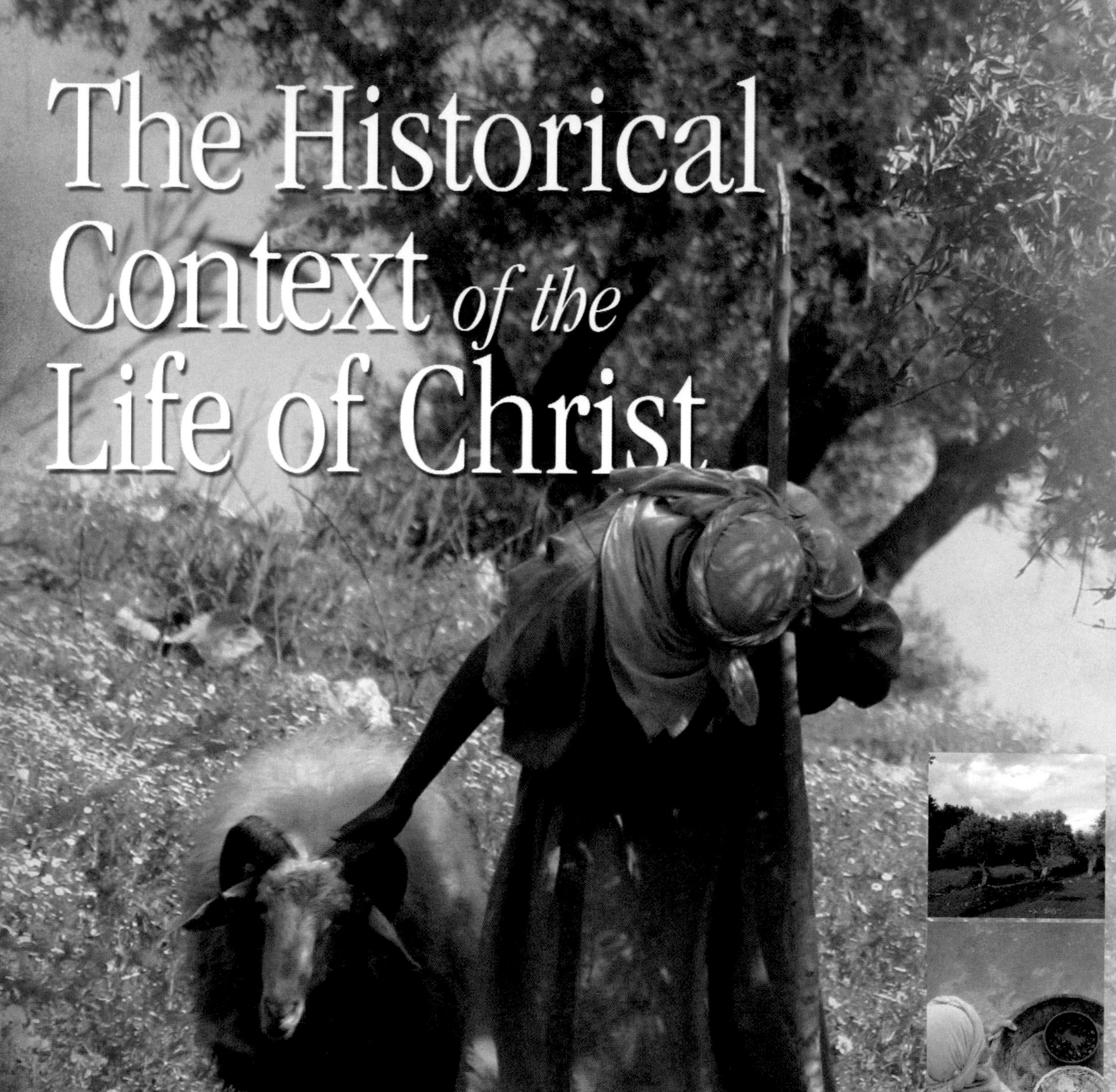

CHAPTER 1

The stories of Jesus' life, particularly those that tell of his miracles, can sometimes make his life sound more like that of a storybook super-hero than the historical account of a person who lived in a real place and time. Yet, as surely as Jesus was supernatural, he was also human; this is his mystery and his glory. He was born a baby and grew up day-by-day and year-by-year. He probably labored with his father in the carpenter shop. He received criticism as well as praise. At times his family misunderstood him, and even had deep concern for him.

Like all of us, Jesus had to deal with politics and weather, with sickness and hunger, with good times and bad times. He attended weddings and ate dinner with friends. He wept. He laughed. The very people he came to this world to help sometimes worked against him. His best friends didn't always come through when he needed them. He faced the same extremes of life that we all face: that is part of the point of his journey on earth. The New Testament says that because he faced the same temptations we all do, he has compassion for our struggles (Hebrews 4:15).

Jesus Christ lived in the first half of the first century. His work carried him between Judea to the south and Galilee to the north. These areas can roughly be defined as the land area between the Mediterranean Sea on the west and the Jordan River, which empties into the Dead Sea, on the east. During Jesus' life this area was under Roman occupation.

Jesus was a Jewish man. His culture was typical of the Middle East, though the religion of Islam had not yet been founded in his time. While in the Western world artists have often depicted him as having Caucasian features, his physical appearance would likely have been much closer to that of a modern-day Palestinian than a European or North American.

To understand the life of Christ, we must enter into the spirit of the place, time, and culture in which he lived. We must seek to walk in his shoes—or, to prove the point—in his sandals. The religious climate, the political climate, and even the geography of Judea and Galilee all play a significant role in the story of Jesus.

First-Century Judea

Stepping back in time 2,000 years to the small, rural villages of Judea would be a shock to those of us who have grown up in modern metropolitan areas, but some things haven't changed. Jerusalem was even then a capital city, buzzing with gossip and political intrigue. The town elders, whose roles were similar to those of today's city council members, were found at the gates of the city, hobnobbing with the residents, passing judgment on current political issues, and campaigning for the new and improved. At the Damascus Gate young and old wove their way through the narrow city streets, children played, and parents set up shop for another day of vending their wares. The city was alive with the hustle and bustle of a county-seat market town.

Model of old Jerusalem

Panoramic view of Galilee, Israel

After Jesus had finished instructing his twelve disciples, he left and began teaching and preaching in the towns. Matthew 11:1

Religion played a major role in daily life. The religious leaders of the day often confronted Jesus about his teachings and challenged his authority (see Matthew 11:20–24, 21:23–27, and 23:1–36). This group would have included the chief priests and scribes and elders, Pharisees, Saducees, and Herodians—highly visible in the town's courtyards and synagogues. Robust discourse could be heard as they responded to questions about the *Torah* (the first five books of the Old Testament, attributed to Moses), and the practical commentary of those texts that became known as the Talmud.

The surrounding region of Judea, in contrast to the urban oasis of Jerusalem, was a typical hard working, agrarian community. The residents of small villages like Bethlehem and Bethany weren't concerned with the doings of politicians and priests: here in the countryside there was work to do. The cost of living in a small town like Cana of Galilee was not what it was in the big city, and folks then, like now, busied themselves with making a living today and hoping for a better life for their children tomorrow. The lives of such simple farmers would change little over the centuries; the story of the Jewish dairyman Tevye, the lead figure of the musical comedy *Fiddler on the Roof*, is set in Russia in 1905, yet it reflects in many ways the lives of the Jews of Jesus' time.

The Geography of Jesus'

Since the beginning of recorded history, Israel has been a strategic crossroads, a kind of land-bridge, that links Egypt and Saudi Arabia to the south with the nations known today as Syria, Turkey, Iraq, and Iran to the north. Over the centuries, soldiers of many different conquering empires crisscrossed this small sliver of land as they marched to war.

Jerusalem, Jerusalem! . . . I have often wanted to gather your people, as a hen gathers her chicks under her wings. But you wouldn't let me. Now your temple will be deserted. You won't see me again until the time when you say, "Blessed is the one who comes in the name of the Lord."
Luke 13:34–35

The city of Jerusalem, set on a mountain, is the crown jewel of the nation of Israel. Its location, the Book of Revelation (21:2) tells us, is the site where a new Jerusalem will come down out of heaven and rest on a mountaintop. Jerusalem is referred to in Ezekiel 5:5, where the holy city is described as the center of the nations. Jewish scholars tell us that this reference to the center is neither a mathematical term nor a geographic term. The term indicates that this place is at the navel, or point of origin, of all human history and destiny.

Heavenly Jerusalem.
Early Christian mosaic. 5th CE.
Location: S. Maria Maggiore, Rome, Italy

Homeland

Israel is a tiny nation that encompasses only 8,500 square miles of land. Roughly the size of New Jersey, it is located in the region of southwest Asia known as the Middle East. Its neighbors are Egypt and the African continent to the west and south, respectively, Lebanon and Syria to the north, and Jordan to the east. With the beautiful Mediterranean Sea to the west and the Jordan River on its eastern border, this "land of milk and honey," as the Old Testament calls it, sounds as if it is blessed with rich resources of water. But that is not the case, for the Negev desert in Israel's south constitutes 60 percent of the nation's land area.

Israel's primary water source, the Jordan River—where John the Baptist inaugurated Jesus' ministry—begins as a tiny trickle in the mountains of Lebanon and then empties into the Sea of Galilee on its course south toward the lowest point on the face of the earth, the Dead Sea. Sodom and Gomorrah were cities located on the coast of the Dead Sea in the days of Abraham and his nephew Lot. But according to the story recorded in Genesis 18:16–19:29, God's judgment fell upon the occupants of the twin cities, whose immoral ways were well known, and the water became a saline solution that even today allows tourists to float on top of the surface of the water. The other chemical characteristic of this area is sulfuric rock—otherwise known as brimstone.

The Dead Sea, Israel

The Social and Cultural Climate

The cultural climate of the land of Israel in Jesus' day can be summed up in two words: domination and determination. For 1800 years before Christ was born, the Jewish people had been dominated: first by the Egyptians, then by the Assyrians, then by the Babylonians, the Medo-Persians, the Greeks and, finally, the Romans.

A century and a half later, in the time of Jesus, Israel was a province of the Roman empire, called Judea. The Jews were not a free people; they were subjects of Rome. They lived in a world of fearful anticipation, aware that brutal taxes or sanctions might be imposed upon them at any moment—by a government that ignored their significant religious heritage. Their own form of government had developed over the centuries: at first eminent judges ruled the Jews, then a single king, then many kings. In Jesus' time, the Sanhedrin, a group of religious leaders, served as the Jews' representative body—but they did so only at the behest of the true political ruler of Judea, the Roman Empire.

Without experiencing it firsthand, it's difficult to understand the daily lives of the citizens of Judea, a nation occupied by a foreign power. Taxes and many laws were imposed by a faraway government, and no entrepreneurial endeavor could be undertaken without the explicit permission of Judea's imperial overlords.

As this series of dominating powers traveled through the tiny land-bridge of Israel, the Jewish people rallied together to preserve their cultural heritage. They observed seven biblical festivals annually to help them remember their history, sustain their identity, and encourage their stability. Chapter 23 of the book of Leviticus in the Old Testament is dedicated to an explanation of these seven feasts. They are divided into two categories: springtime events and fall events. The first four are ***Passover***, ***Unleavened Bread***, ***First Fruits***, and ***Pentecost***. Passover is an agricultural and seasonal celebration. It is followed the next day with the Feast of Unleavened Bread (Hag HaMatzot), a seven-day event.

The ***Passover*** feast began as the celebration of the annual barley harvest, but it was expanded to become a reenactment of the Exodus of the Israelites who escaped Egyptian slavery. The celebration included going to the temple and sacrificing a lamb.

The Feast of Unleavened Bread (Hag HaMatzot) reminded the people of God's command to bake quickly and prepare to leave in haste. The joint celebration of the Passover and the Feast of Unleavened Bread was the first of the three major pilgrimages the Hebrews would celebrate in a calendar year. (The others included the Feast of Booths in the fall and the spring Harvest festival [Pentecost/Shavu'ot].)

First Fruits was the symbolic waving of the first fruits of the barley harvest—a promise of a strong crop leading to a year of health and prosperity.

Pentecost (Shavu'ot), the wheat harvest festival, was expanded to be the reminder of God's giving of the Law to Moses on Mt. Sinai.

The final three sacred feasts were held in the fall of the year. ***The Feast of Trumpets*** (Rosh Hashanah) began a ten-day period of penitence, symbolizing the sins of Adam, the sins of the children of Israel, and the personal and corporate sins of the current population. Trumpets blasted all day in a fashion reminiscent of today's tornado sirens, attracting the attention of the people. ***The Day of Atonement*** (Yom Kippur) was a ritual of purification directed to the land, the temple, and the people. ***The Feast of Booths***, or Tabernacles (Sukkot), was a symbolic reenactment of the Israelites' forty years of wandering in the desert, a time of nomadic conditions remembered by living in tents.

The cultural impact of these seven observances could be likened to seven county fairs every year. The bond they created in the community was so adhesive that, despite their later dispersions and persecutions, the people of Israel remained deeply connected to their cultural traditions.

Golden Passover Plate

A QUOTE FROM THE BIBLE

LEVITICUS 23:4–8

Passover is another time when you must come together to worship me, and it must be celebrated on the evening of the fourteenth day of the first month of each year. The Festival of Thin Bread begins on the fifteenth day of that same month; it lasts seven days, and during this time you must honor me by eating bread made without yeast. On the first day of this festival you must rest from your work and come together for worship. Each day of this festival you must offer sacrifices. Then on the final day you must once again rest from your work and come together for worship.

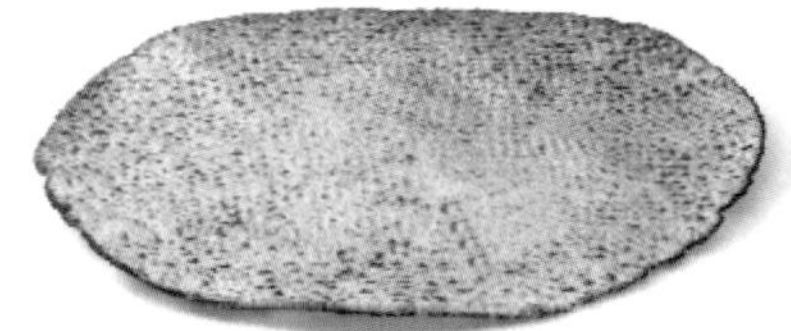

The Political Climate of First-Century Judea

Herod the Great died in 4 BC, after ruling Judea for thirty-three years. He was somewhat of a puppet king, or, as the Romans referred to him, a "client king." Herod's bloodline as an Idumean, or Edomite, gave him enough political clout to be deemed a ruler of Judea, but it did not guarantee him the acceptance or loyalty of the Jewish people. Even so, during his reign, Judea prospered economically and Israel's borders were extended.

At Herod's death his kingdom was divided among his three sons, who became known as tetrarchs (meaning "a quarter of the kingdom"). These sons ruled during Jesus' lifetime.

In the first-century Jewish community, the leaders of the religious community also served as political leaders. Although the region was under Roman authority, the Jews were allowed to govern themselves, to a certain extent. Several key groups made up the political structure that listened to Jesus' claims and passed judgment upon them. In Mark 11:27, we learn that during the last week of Jesus' ministry, the chief priests, the scribes, and the elders came to him and challenged his authority. Mark 12:13 tells us that the Pharisees and Herodians were sent to him in order to trap him. And Mark 12:18 reports that the Sadducees came to him, badgering him with assaulting questions. The goal of the leaders was to trap Jesus, through his words or deeds, in a crime that would result in the death sentence.

A number of different groups of leaders of the Jewish community played a role in the last week of Jesus' life.

The ruins of Masada

Magi Before King Herod (antebaptistry). 1343–54, Byzantine mosaic. Location: S. Marco, Venice, Italy

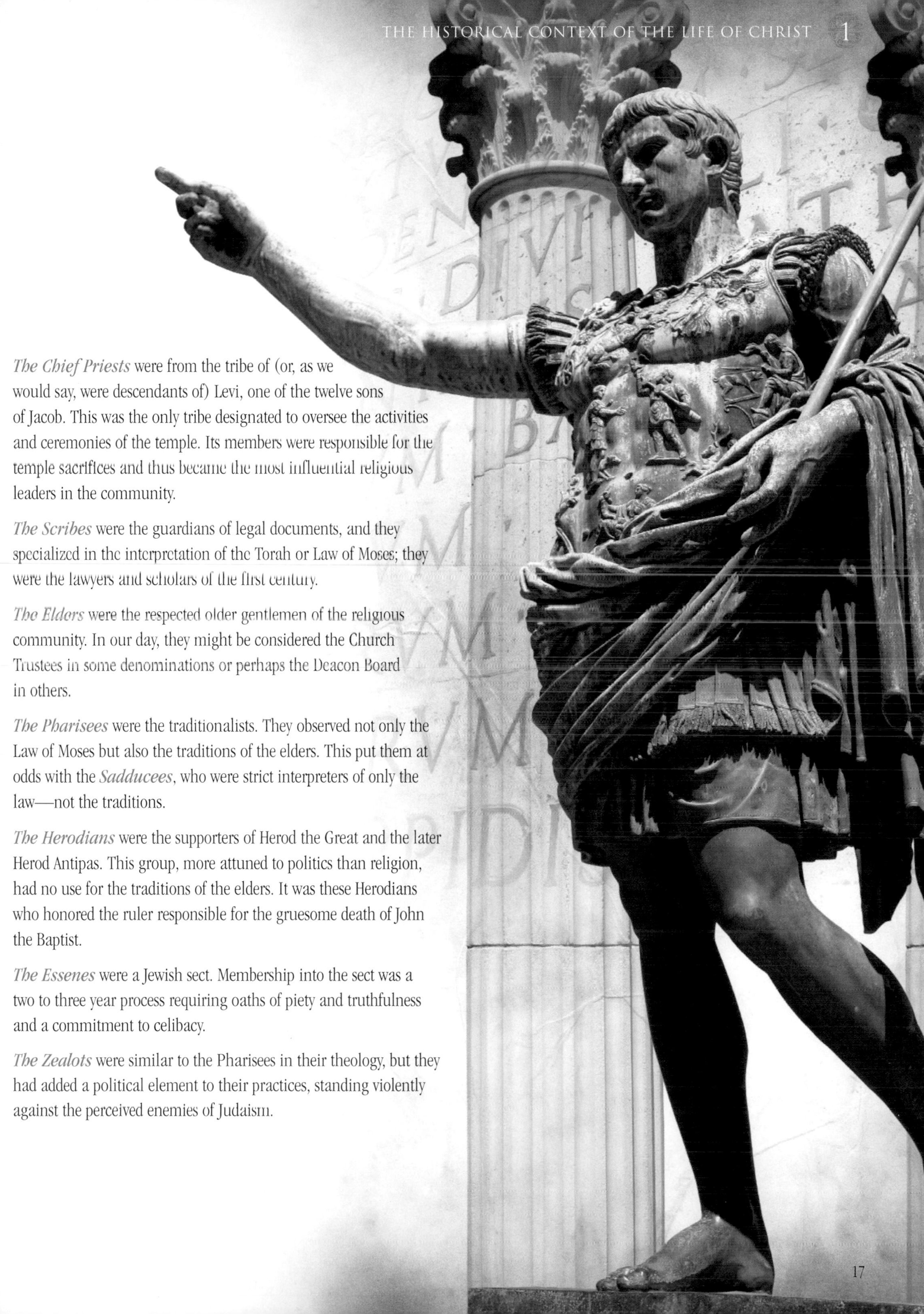

The Chief Priests were from the tribe of (or, as we would say, were descendants of) Levi, one of the twelve sons of Jacob. This was the only tribe designated to oversee the activities and ceremonies of the temple. Its members were responsible for the temple sacrifices and thus became the most influential religious leaders in the community.

The Scribes were the guardians of legal documents, and they specialized in the interpretation of the Torah or Law of Moses; they were the lawyers and scholars of the first century.

The Elders were the respected older gentlemen of the religious community. In our day, they might be considered the Church Trustees in some denominations or perhaps the Deacon Board in others.

The Pharisees were the traditionalists. They observed not only the Law of Moses but also the traditions of the elders. This put them at odds with the *Sadducees*, who were strict interpreters of only the law—not the traditions.

The Herodians were the supporters of Herod the Great and the later Herod Antipas. This group, more attuned to politics than religion, had no use for the traditions of the elders. It was these Herodians who honored the ruler responsible for the gruesome death of John the Baptist.

The Essenes were a Jewish sect. Membership into the sect was a two to three year process requiring oaths of piety and truthfulness and a commitment to celibacy.

The Zealots were similar to the Pharisees in their theology, but they had added a political element to their practices, standing violently against the perceived enemies of Judaism.

The Religious World of

The prevailing influences in Judea and Galilee in the first century were philosophy, government, and religion—Greek philosophy, Roman government, and Jewish religion. Philosophy had never been better explained than by the Greeks. Government had never been better structured than by the Romans. And no pagan world religion was as devout and ceremonial as the Jewish faith.

By the first century, faith in the God and religion of Israel was 1400 years old. The Jewish people worshiped in the temple and studied the Law of Moses. They honored and practiced the ceremonies and traditions of their ancestors, especially those relating to the education and rearing of children.

The temple in Jerusalem was the center of Jewish religious life. There were several temples built throughout Jewish history. Herod the Great, who ruled Judea at the time of Jesus' birth, was known for his admiration of Roman culture and his great buildings. In 19 BC, he began building the grand Jerusalem temple where Jesus would have worshiped. Construction on this temple continued throughout and beyond Jesus' life in Judea, until around AD 64. Today, the western Wailing Wall is what remains of this temple.

One of the primary functions of the temple in Jerusalem was to provide a place for animal sacrifices overseen by the priests. It also served as a center for judicial and community life. Worship was conducted there, as well as prayers, the collection of tithes, and festivals.

The New Testament writer Luke described Jesus' religious practice this way: "Jesus went back to Nazareth, where he had been brought up, and as usual he went to the synagogue on the Sabbath. When he stood up to read from the Scriptures, he was given the book of Isaiah the prophet. He opened it and read, 'The Lord's Spirit has come to me . . . '" (Luke 4:16–18).

There was one central Jewish temple, but there were synagogues or meeting houses throughout the Roman Empire. These synagogues functioned as teaching, worship, and community centers. The temple was the high and holy place where the full attention of the priests and the people was to fulfill the ceremonial laws of God. The synagogue would have been the place where marriages were performed, parties were held, and intellectual dialogue took place. Jesus would have honored the temple and its ceremonies. He also would have gone to the synagogue to reach out to the common people who were desperately looking for the voice of God and the Messiah.

Jerusalem dating from the time of the Second Temple

First-Century Judea

Table of show bread

The Jewish faith had these earmarks:

Monotheism ▪ Their belief in one God set the Jews apart from the main religions of the Greco-Roman world that worshiped multiple gods or idols.

God's covenant with Abraham, the great ancestor of the Jews ▪ An essential part of Jewish history was the promise God made to the then childless Abraham that his descendants would become a great nation.

Adherence to the *Torah*, or Law of Moses ▪ *Torah*, a Hebrew word, means "teaching" or "instruction." The term Torah can refer to the specific commandments given through Moses, but it can also refer generally to the first five books of the Bible: Genesis, Exodus, Leviticus, Numbers, and Deuteronomy.

The shofar was employed in religious ceremonies, in processions, or in the orchestra as an accompaniment to the song of praise.

HEROD

Herod the Great ruled the land of Israel during the time of Jesus' birth. Called "King Herod," he had been appointed to his office by the Senate in Rome.

A paranoid ruler, Herod maintained power at times by violence. He executed one of his wives and murdered his sister's husband. When he felt threatened by his nephew, he marshaled his troops against him. He also married his own niece to secure his power. With this background, it is not surprising that he issued a death sentence to a few baby boys living in the small town of Bethlehem—the town which was the purported home of a newly-born king (Matthew 2:5).

While known for his use of strong force, Herod was also recognized as a master architect. Herod rebuilt the temple in Jerusalem, expanded the city walls, built a fortress at Masada, expanded the country's water supplies, and built a number of beautiful buildings throughout Israel that still stand (at least in part) today.

At Herod's death, the country was divided between his three sons and each ruled over his own region (as indicated on the map).

Israel in Jesus' Time
Land ruled by Herod the Great
Land ruled by Herod Archelaus
Land ruled by Herod Philip
Land ruled by Herod Antipas
0 10 20 30 Miles
0 10 20 30 40 Km
PHOENICIA
Mount Hermon
Tyre
Caesarea Philippi
GALILEE
Ptolemais
Capernaum
Bethsaida?
Gennesaret
Gergesa?
Cana
Magdala?
Tiberias
Sea of Galilee
Sepphoris
Nazareth
Gadara
Nain
DECAPOLIS
Caesarea
Salim?
Aenon?
SHARON
Sebaste (Samaria)
Gerasa
Mount Gerizim
Sychar?
SAMARIA
Jabbok River
Antipatris
Joppa
PEREA
Arimathea?
Jordan River
Lydda
Ephraim?
Jericho
Emmaus?
Jerusalem
Azotus
Qumran
Bethlehem
JUDEA
Dead Sea
Machaerus
Hebron
Gaza
IDUMEA
Arnon River
Masada
Beersheba
NABATEA

CHAPTER 2

JESUS

The New Testament presents Jesus as the Messiah, God-in-the-flesh. It's a mystery, but Christians believe the Bible teaches that Jesus was both fully God and fully human. He was God's Son, and yet he was a person. Specifically, he was a first-century, middle-eastern, Jewish man.

Jesus grew up as we do: from baby to child, from boy to man. His was a fully human experience. Some Christians believe he was not an only child and that he had brothers and sisters (Mark 6:3). His father was a carpenter (Matthew 13:55), which at that time probably implied a builder who worked not only with wood, but with a variety of materials. Jesus was referred to as a carpenter, too (Mark 6:3). As would have been common in that day, he probably learned his father's trade.

According to the Gospel accounts, Jesus had many friends and acquaintances. He ate supper with the friends of Matthew and was criticized for it, and was even accused of drinking to excess (Matthew 11:18–19). He felt emotions—including anger (Mark 3:5); legitimate anxiety and anguish over difficulties (Luke 22:44); sadness and even weeping (Luke 19:41). He was tempted, just as people today are tempted (Matthew 4:1–11; Hebrews 4:15).

From the biblical texts we learn that Jesus also knew honor. In his culture, one way in which a person's honor was determined was by how well he debated with the leaders of that time. Thus, in the Gospels, when Jesus repeatedly confronted the religious leaders, even confounded them, those who saw and heard the interchanges were increasingly impressed with his spiritual authority (Luke 4:31–32). Understanding this about Jesus' culture also reveals how distinctive his message would have been—that true honor comes from serving others, not through overpowering or confounding one's adversaries.

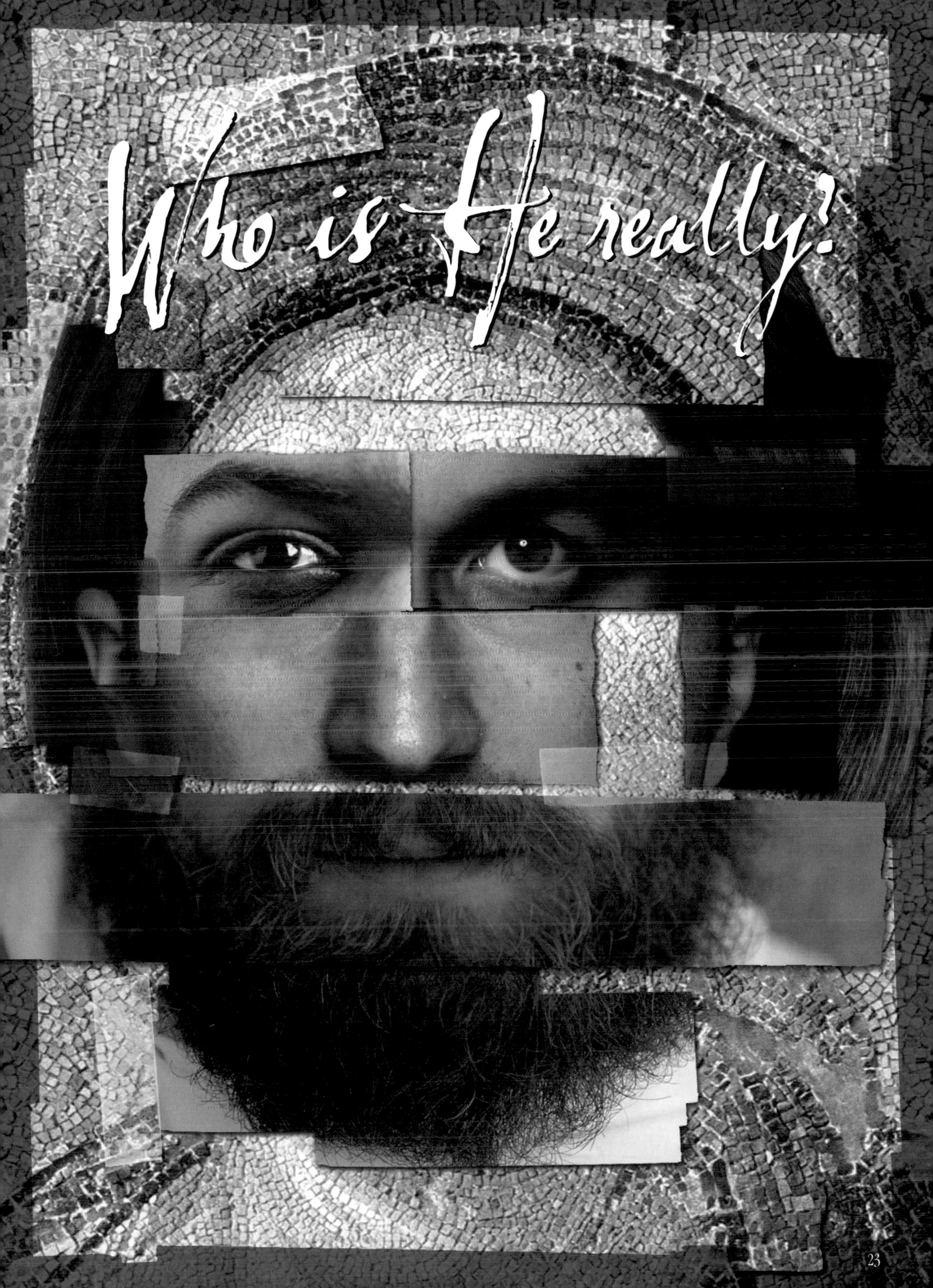
Who is He really?

MEETING JESUS

JEWISH MAN OF MYSTERY

We know from the Bible that Jesus fully understood the human experience. We can paint a further probable picture of his life from what we now know of the usual customs of first-century Palestine and the typical experience of a Jewish man in the Roman province of Judea.

Jesus' extended family would have been as much a part of his life as his immediate family. He was raised to honor his parents, and the responsibility to care for them in their old age would have been emphasized as he grew up. As a young man, he would have been trained at home and at the synagogue, studying the Law of Moses.

He ate two meals a day, at noon and at the end of the day. The menu may have included bread, vegetables, fruit, fish, and milk products, including yogurt and cheese. Meat was served mostly at holidays. Honey and dates were the most common sweetening agents for food. He would have eaten on a mat on the floor, dipping bread into a common bowl with the rest of the family—using his right hand. Water was unsafe, so it was usually mixed with wine.

He would have slept on a mat on the floor beside other family members. He would have attended large weddings and feasts with them as well. Among his family, hospitality, even to strangers, would have been highly valued.

He likely had a beard and longer hair than his Greek and Roman counterparts. He would have worn a knee-length garment made of linen called a tunic. It would have been tied around his waist with a sash. For cooler days, he probably added a cloak, perhaps made of wool. When he wore sandals, they were most likely made of leather.

His was a culture in which identity was founded more in the group than in the individual. A person's family and nationality were essential aspects of his or her life. On an individual basis, the esteem of one's fellow citizens determined a person's sense of honor or shame. What wealth is to modern capitalist cultures, honor was to the first-century Mediterranean culture.

Head of Christ
17th Century. Oil on panel.
Rembrandt Harmensz van Rijn (1606–1669) (attributed to).
Philadelphia Museum of Art, Philadelphia, Pennsylvania, U.S.A.

Who do you say I AM?

Jesus spoke with authority that inspired the masses. Not only did he stir hearts, but he affected lives. Jesus' words changed lives, healed the sick, raised the dead. The Bible recounts that Jesus' words were so powerful because he was more than just a man.

MARK 8:27–30

Jesus and his disciples went to the villages near the town of Caesarea Philippi. As they were walking along, he asked them, "What do people say about me?"

The disciples answered, "Some say you are John the Baptist or maybe Elijah. Others say you are one of the prophets."

Then Jesus asked them, "But who do you say I am?"
"You are the Messiah!" Peter replied.
Jesus warned the disciples not to tell anyone about him.

"I AM TRYING HERE TO PREVENT ANYONE SAYING THE REALLY FOOLISH THING THAT PEOPLE OFTEN SAY ABOUT HIM: 'I'M READY TO ACCEPT JESUS AS A GREAT MORAL TEACHER, BUT I DON'T ACCEPT HIS CLAIM TO BE GOD.' THAT IS THE ONE THING WE MUST NOT SAY. A MAN WHO SAID THE SORT OF THINGS JESUS SAID WOULD NOT BE A GREAT MORAL TEACHER. HE WOULD EITHER BE A LUNATIC—ON A LEVEL WITH THE MAN WHO SAYS HE IS A POACHED EGG—OR ELSE HE WOULD BE THE DEVIL OF HELL. YOU MUST MAKE YOUR CHOICE. EITHER THIS MAN WAS, AND IS, THE SON OF GOD: OR ELSE A MADMAN OR SOMETHING WORSE. YOU CAN SHUT HIM UP FOR A FOOL, YOU CAN SPIT AT HIM AND KILL HIM AS A DEMON; OR YOU CAN FALL AT HIS FEET AND CALL HIM LORD AND GOD. BUT LET US NOT COME WITH ANY PATRONIZING NONSENSE ABOUT HIS BEING A GREAT HUMAN TEACHER. HE HAS NOT LEFT THAT OPEN TO US. HE DID NOT INTEND TO."

—C.S. Lewis, *Mere Christianity*, revised edition, New York, Macmillan/Collier, 1952.

TEACHING, MISSION, AND REVOLUTION

Jesus taught much about the kingdom of God. His message, like John the Baptist's, was an urgent call for each of us to repent of our sins—not because the kingdom of God was coming eventually, but because the kingdom of God had already come, in his mission. In this sense, God's kingdom was not a worldly empire based in a given time and place, but the spiritual reality that God is in control of our destinies.

Jesus' mission was misunderstood by many. He had not come to make Israel politically victorious over her enemies. He had not come to reign over a nation with the royal trappings of an army and castle. He had come to serve, to suffer, and to sacrifice himself (Matthew 20:28). He had come to show humanity how to live as members of a kingdom of the Spirit, God's kingdom (Matthew 5:2–12).

Jesus' work and words were revolutionary because he turned his back on the status quo of his culture. Though he honored the commandments of God and many of the traditions of his people, like many of the ancient prophets before him, he seemed to abhor those who practiced religion for religion's sake, by rote or for show. He confronted the hypocrisy of some of the religious leaders and openly disregarded traditions that were inconsistent with the spirit of the law (Matthew 23:1–36).

And most revolutionary of all, as Jesus' ministry progressed, he revealed more and more of his true identity—he proclaimed that he was the promised Messiah, Immanuel, which means "God with us."

The kingdom of heaven is like what happens when someone finds a treasure hidden in a field and buries it again. Such a person is happy and goes and sells everything in order to buy that field.

The kingdom of heaven is like what happens when a shop owner is looking for fine pearls. After finding a very valuable one, the owner goes and sells everything in order to buy that pearl.

Matthew 13:44–46

Christ Crowned with Thorns. (wood)
Filipino School (20th Century)
Boltin Picture Library/The Bridgeman Art Library

PROPHECIES, MIRACLES, AND HEALED LIVES

Jesus' life was filled with wonders and miracles. Certain details of his life held true to ancient prophecies of the Messiah that were written or spoken centuries before Jesus lived. He proved his power over nature by calming storms (Mark 4:35–40); over death by disrupting funerals and even gravesites (Mark 5:35–42; John 11:32–44); over sickness by bringing health (Mark 5:25–34). He performed some of these miracles with just a single word. He performed others from a remote location (Matthew 8:5–13).

While Jesus desired faith from his followers that did not rely on his supernatural feats, his miracles played an important part in revealing his authority as God's Son.

An Old Testament prophecy is found in Isaiah 35:3–6 that Jesus' followers applied to Jesus and to the good Jesus would bring to those who believed in him:

Here is a message for all
who are weak, trembling,
and worried:
"Cheer up! Don't be afraid.
Your God is coming
to punish your enemies.
God will take revenge on them
and rescue you."

The blind will see,
and the ears of the deaf
will be healed.
Those who were lame
will leap around like deer;
tongues once silent
will shout for joy.
Water will rush
through the desert.

A QUOTE FROM THE BIBLE

MATTHEW 11:2–6

John was in prison when he heard what Christ was doing. So John sent some of his followers to ask Jesus, "Are you the one we should be looking for? Or must we wait for someone else?"

Jesus answered, "Go and tell John what you have heard and seen. The blind are now able to see, and the lame can walk. People with leprosy are being healed, and the deaf can hear. The dead are raised to life, and the poor are hearing the good news. God will bless everyone who doesn't reject me because of what I do."

Christ Before Pilate.
Undated. Pastel.
Beck, Walter (1864–1954)
Location: Smithsonian American Art Museum, Washington, DC, U.S.A.

THE GREAT "I AM"

(EGO EIMI)

The apostle John states, "Jesus worked many other miracles for his disciples, and not all of them are written in this book. But these are written so that you will put your faith in Jesus as the Messiah and the Son of God. If you have faith in him, you will have true life." (John 20:30-31)

We can see that John's aim is two-fold. On one hand, he seeks to demonstrate that Jesus is "the Messiah, the Son of God." On the other, he wants people to know the true identity of Jesus, so that "you will have true life."

When God commanded Moses to lead Israel out of slavery in Egypt, Moses asked what God's name was. God replied, "tell them that the LORD, whose name is 'I Am,' has sent you" (Exodus 3:13–15). Jesus shows that he has been in God's plan from the beginning when he said: "even before Abraham was, I was, and I am." (John 8:58)

In John's Gospel, Jesus uses the term "I am" to connect himself to aspects of God's nature and to identify himself as the one who

- supplies all needs
- brings the knowledge about God to all people
- is the way for people to find God and become God's people
- promises that all who believe in him will have eternal life
- invites everyone to share in the common life as the new people of God

I AM the bread that gives life!

I tell you for certain that everyone who has faith in me has eternal life.

I am the bread that gives life! Your ancestors ate manna in the desert, and later they died. But the bread from heaven has come down, so that no one who eats it will ever die. I am that bread from heaven! Everyone who eats it will live forever. My flesh is the life-giving bread that I give to the people of this world.

JOHN 6:47–51

I AM the light for the world!

Once again Jesus spoke to the people. This time he said, "I am the light for the world! Follow me, and you won't be walking in the dark. You will have the light that gives life."

JOHN 8:12

I AM the gate for the sheep.

Jesus said: "I tell you for certain that I am the gate for the sheep. Everyone who came before me was a thief or a robber, and the sheep did not listen to any of them. I am the gate. All who come in through me will be saved. Through me they will come and go and find pasture. A thief comes only to rob, kill, and destroy. I came so everyone would have life, and have it fully."

JOHN 10:7–10

I AM the good shepherd.

I am the good shepherd, and the good shepherd gives up his life for his sheep. Hired workers are not like the shepherd. They don't own the sheep, and when they see a wolf coming, they run off and leave the sheep. Then the wolf attacks and scatters the flock. Hired workers run away because they don't care about the sheep.

I am the good shepherd. I know my sheep, and they know me. Just as the Father knows me, I know the Father, and I give up my life for my sheep. I have other sheep that are not in this sheep pen. I must also bring them together, when they hear my voice. Then there will be one flock of sheep and one shepherd.

JOHN 10:11–16

I AM the one who raises the dead to life!

Jesus then said *to Martha*, "I am the one who raises the dead to life! Everyone who has faith in me will live, even if they die. And everyone who lives because of faith in me will never really die. Do you believe this?"

"Yes, Lord!" she replied. "I believe that you are Christ, the Son of God. You are the one we hoped would come into the world."

JOHN 11:25–27

I AM the way, the truth, and the life!

I am the way, the truth, and the life! ... Without me, no one can go to the Father.

JOHN 14:6

I AM the vine.

I am the vine, and you are the branches. If you stay joined to me, and I stay joined to you, then you will produce lots of fruit. But you cannot do anything without me. If you don't stay joined to me, you will be thrown away. You will be like dry branches that are gathered up and burned in a fire. Stay joined to me and let my teachings become part of you. Then you can pray for whatever you want, and your prayer will be answered.

JOHN 15:5–7

Historical
INFORMATION

CHAPTER 3

THERE ARE HISTORICAL REFERENCES TO THE LIFE OF JESUS OUTSIDE THE BIBLE, AND THERE ARE ALSO EARLY MANUSCRIPTS THAT WERE NOT INCLUDED IN THE BOOKS THAT FORM THE OLD AND NEW TESTAMENTS. BUT THE EARLY CHURCH DECIDED THAT THE MOST RELIABLE STORIES OF JESUS' LIFE AND WORK ARE FOUND IN THE FIRST FOUR BOOKS OF THE NEW TESTAMENT—THE GOSPELS ACCORDING TO MATTHEW, MARK, LUKE, AND JOHN.

These are not actual biographies as we think of them today, nor are they exhaustive, scholarly treatises. Perhaps they are best described as theological documents that tell us about Jesus' teachings and his ministry from a particular perspective. Their authors were not simply describing his life; they were also making a point about the significance of that life—and its conclusion in death and resurrection. For instance, John's Gospel presents Jesus as the preexistent Word made flesh, while Mark's Gospel depicts Jesus in a very different way. Both Gospels present valid theological portraits of Jesus, but with different goals, even when they describe the same event.

These documents have been read and reread through the centuries in the hope they will provide new understanding and new perspectives on Jesus' life and mission. They offer answers even as they leave us with questions, and so they keep us eternally searching for their meaning.

Understanding the Gospels from the perspective of the original writers and readers of these documents is crucial to our interpretation of them. We must ask ourselves: What would a first-century seeker of the truth make of Matthew's version of the Sermon on the Mount, or Luke's detailed account of Jesus' birth?

The latter part of the first century was a scramble, a time of enormous change and challenge. The Jewish nation was scrambling to preserve its identity, as its people faced destruction and dispersion. The new Jewish Christians were scrambling to make sense of the new faith they had been given without the benefit of the collected New Testament writings—which were still being created in their midst—to guide them. Those in the non-Jewish world were scambling to understand the message of this Jewish Messiah. Those who considered it their responsibility to carry on Jesus' message and his work—the people who had been closest to him during his life—were scrambling to figure out how to organize themselves, how to live and worship together as a church, and how to proclaim Christ's promise of salvation.

When we look back at the information written during this tumultuous time, the effect can seem similar to finding a corked bottle floating on the ocean with a message scribbled by shaking hands in the midst of a fray. We uncork that bottle when we reread the story of Jesus.

A QUOTE FROM THE BIBLE

JOHN 21:25

Jesus did many other things. If they were all written in books, I don't suppose there would be room enough in the whole world for all the books.

THE GOSPELS

WE LEARN ABOUT THE LIFE OF JESUS FROM THE FIRST FOUR BOOKS OF THE NEW TESTAMENT—MATTHEW, MARK, LUKE, AND JOHN—WHICH ARE ATTRIBUTED TO MEN WHO LIVED IN THE FIRST CENTURY. EACH GOSPEL PROVIDES A UNIQUE WRITTEN VERSION OF THE LIFE-GIVING MINISTRY AND MESSAGE OF JESUS CHRIST.

SINCE THE GOSPELS WERE WRITTEN DOWN IN THE FIRST CENTURY, LONG BEFORE PRINTING PRESSES AND OTHER MODERN TECHNOLOGIES, THE STORIES THEY RECORD WERE LIKELY FIRST SHARED BY WORD OF MOUTH. THEY ARE LIFE-CHANGING STORIES THAT INCLUDE MIRACLES, PARABLES, CONVERSATIONS, AND FORMAL TEACHING. EVEN TWO THOUSAND YEARS LATER, THEY RETAIN THEIR ABILITY TO STRETCH US—TO FORCE US TO CONTEMPLATE FORGIVENESS, PEACE, AND LOVE IN A RADICAL WAY. THEY PRESENT US WITH A PARADOX: A PERSON WHO WAS BOTH FULLY GOD AND FULLY MAN. THEY DESCRIBE HOW THAT PERSON CAME TO SAVE THE WORLD AND HOW, IN THE PROCESS, HE DIED BRUTALLY ON A CROSS AND, ULTIMATELY, ROSE FROM THE GRAVE. SOME OF THE STORIES CAN SEEM UNBELIEVABLE, YET EVEN SO THEY RESONATE WITH INNER TRUTH.

The Gospels

THE FOUR GOSPELS TELL OF JESUS' LIFE ON EARTH, A STORY THAT IS NOT SEPARATE FROM THE REST OF THE BIBLE, BUT IN FACT CAN BEST BE UNDERSTOOD WITHIN THE CONTEXT OF THE ENTIRE BIBLE. THEY OFTEN DRAW ON THE OLD TESTAMENT TO EMPHASIZE THE FULFILLMENT OF JUDAISM'S PROPHECIES AND THE RESTORATION OF HUMANKIND'S RELATIONSHIP WITH GOD THAT WAS BROKEN IN THE EARLIEST HISTORY OF HUMANITY. THOUGH THE BOOKS AREN'T EXHAUSTIVE BIOGRAPHIES OF JESUS, THEY PROVIDE US WITH ENOUGH STORIES, WONDERS, TEACHINGS, AND INCIDENTS FOR A LIFETIME OF CONTEMPLATION.

THE FIRST THREE GOSPELS OVERLAP, SHARING MANY OF THE SAME STORIES OF JESUS' LIFE. THESE THREE ARE OFTEN REFERRED TO AS THE SYNOPTIC GOSPELS (FROM A GREEK WORD THAT MEANS "VIEWED TOGETHER"). THE FOURTH, JOHN'S GOSPEL, TAKES A DIFFERENT, SOMEWHAT MORE PHILOSOPHICAL APPROACH TO DESCRIBING THE LIFE OF CHRIST. HERE'S A LOOK AT WHAT MAKES EACH OF THE GOSPELS UNIQUE.

THE GOSPEL OF MATTHEW

The Gospel according to Matthew emphasizes that Jesus came not to abolish the Law or the Prophets, but to fulfill them (see Matthew 5:17). In a systematic, orderly style, this book describes Jesus Christ as the Jewish Messiah who was foretold by the ancient prophets, linking the works of Jesus to Jewish tradition and scripture. Because Matthew's Gospel contains numerous references to Old Testament prophecies, it is sometimes thought of as the book where "the Old Testament meets the New."

The book starts out by tracing the genealogy of Jesus back to King David, presenting Jesus as a king of God's people. The stories it tells focus on the major themes of Jesus' teaching: ethics, discipleship, the kingdom of heaven, the church, and the final judgment.

The author of this Gospel does not name himself, possibly because he was keen on showing Jesus' place in history rather than establishing his own legacy. Whatever the writer's reason for remaining anonymous, there is some debate among scholars as to who actually wrote this book. The strongest tradition holds that this Gospel was written by the disciple called Matthew, who had been a tax collector. Scholars believe that both the authors of Matthew and Luke probably made use of Mark's Gospel in writing their own accounts.

THE GOSPEL OF MARK

The Gospel according to Mark is told in a fast-paced, dramatic fashion. Concentrating on Jesus' miracles more than his teachings, it portrays Jesus as a Savior who came to encourage and serve his people, the Son of God who made the ultimate sacrifice by dying on the cross. Mark captures the intensity of Jesus' time on earth by crowding one major event immediately on the heels of another. Jesus' power to bring salvation to a broken world is depicted as an irresistible force.

The Gospel according to Mark is believed to be the earliest of the four Gospels. It was probably written for an audience of persecuted Romans who had converted to Christianity. Though the disciple Mark is considered the author, Peter (who would become an early leader in the Church and, according to Roman Catholic tradition, the first Pope) is thought to be the source for much of Mark's vivid detail. And it makes sense that Peter, a disciple who struggled with his own doubts and demons and even denied knowing Jesus on the night before his death, would have been particularly struck by Jesus' willingness to teach by his own example. In Mark, we witness Jesus demonstrating how we can develop our own faith by serving others and placing our confidence in God.

A QUOTE FROM THE BIBLE

MATTHEW 28:18-20

Jesus came to them and said: "I have been given all authority in heaven and on earth! Go to the people of all nations and make them my disciples. Baptize them in the name of the Father, the Son, and the Holy Spirit, and teach them to do everything I have told you. I will be with you always, even until the end of the world."

A QUOTE FROM THE BIBLE

MARK 10:42-45

Jesus called the disciples together and said: "You know that those foreigners who call themselves kings like to order their people around. And their great leaders have full power over the people they rule. But don't act like them. If you want to be great, you must be the servant of all the others. And if you want to be first, you must be everyone's slave. The Son of Man did not come to be a slave master, but a slave who will give his life to rescue many people."

THE GOSPEL OF
LUKE

The Gospel according to Luke takes a serious and sensitive look at Jesus' life through the eyes of an attentive, intuitive people-watcher. According to early tradition, Luke was a Gentile and a doctor who would eventually accompany the apostle Paul on missionary trips. He is the only non-Jewish writer whose work is included in the New Testament. Perhaps because he wrote for a skeptical Greek audience, he emphasizes the eyewitness accounts and careful research behind his work.

More than any other Gospel writer, Luke describes the prominent role that women played in Jesus' ministry. He also depicts the humanity of Jesus, underscoring that the Savior, however divine, was also a man who ate, cried, and slept like all of us. Luke loved details and crafted his narrative carefully. His attention to the smallest incidents anchors his wondrous tale in everyday reality, and that makes it all the more convincing for readers. His Gospel is sometimes called the "Social Gospel" due to its concern for the poor and marginalized.

THE GOSPEL OF
JOHN

John's Gospel begins by offering us a perspective far outside of Jesus' time on earth, in order to show how Jesus, the Christ, the Word of God, is part of God's eternal plan for his creation. The Gospel according to John is a kind of love story, one that illuminates God's desire to call his people back to himself. It is a beautiful and hopeful expression of the new vision of God's heavenly kingdom that was ushered in by Jesus' mission.

John was a disciple and one of Jesus' closest friends. It was John who stood at the foot of the cross and to whom Jesus entrusted the care of his mother. John recklessly abandoned his previous life to devote his life to Jesus, and he encourages his readers to do the same, by introducing Jesus in an intimate way. John helps us understand Jesus as God, a divine being whose presence in history and in our own lives extends beyond his earthly ministry as our Savior.

A QUOTE FROM THE BIBLE

LUKE 1:1-4

Many people have tried to tell the story of what God has done among us. They wrote what we had been told by the ones who were there in the beginning and saw what happened. So I made a careful study of everything and then decided to write and tell you exactly what took place. Honorable Theophilus, I have done this to let you know the truth about what you have heard.

A QUOTE FROM THE BIBLE

JOHN 20:30-31

Jesus worked many other miracles for his disciples, and not all of them are written in this book. But these are written so that you will put your faith in Jesus as the Messiah and the Son of God. If you have faith in him, you will have true life.

The Other Sources

OTHER SOURCES

THE APOCRYPHAL GOSPELS ARE ANY OF THE TEXTS THAT CLAIM TO BE GOSPELS ABOUT JESUS, BUT FOR ONE REASON OR ANOTHER WEREN'T INCLUDED BY EARLY CHRISTIAN AUTHORITIES IN THE TWENTY-SEVEN BOOKS OF THE NEW TESTAMENT. SOME SCHOLARS THINK THESE BOOKS WERE WRITTEN AFTER THE SECOND CENTURY, WELL AFTER JESUS LIVED AND DIED. IF THAT'S THE CASE, IT UNDERMINES THEIR CLAIMS TO HAVING BEEN WRITTEN BY CONTEMPORARIES OF JESUS. OTHERS SUGGEST THE APOCRYPHAL GOSPELS WEREN'T INCLUDED BECAUSE THEY DEVIATE FROM THE REAL MESSAGES AND EVENTS OF JESUS' LIFE, WHICH WOULD BE ESTABLISHED AS ORTHODOX DOCTRINE.

While the four canonical Gospels offer different details of the life of Christ, they are in harmony concerning their main message: that he was both God and man, and that he came into the world to save humankind from our sins. The apocryphal Gospels often tell a different and fanciful story. They include texts whose names you might recognize (especially if you've read the popular novel *The Da Vinci Code*): the *Gospel of Thomas*, the *Gospel of Philip*, and the *Gospel of Nicodemus*. In general, they offer stories about Jesus' childhood, development, and personal life that do not appear in the canonical Gospels. Although many of us are curious about these areas of Jesus' life, these texts are not considered to be trustworthy sources for such information.

ADDITIONAL HISTORICAL SOURCES

A final way we can learn about Jesus is from historical sources beyond both the Bible and the apocryphal Gospels. A court historian for Emperor Vespasian, Flavius Josephus, wrote about "a wise man…called Jesus." Josephus lived from AD 37–97, just after Jesus' death, and his account describes how Jesus, known for his good conduct and virtue, developed a large following among the Roman Jews and was condemned to death by Pilate. He also notes that despite the tragedy of Jesus' death, his disciples did not abandon his message, but instead claimed that Jesus was alive and had appeared to them after his crucifixion. This account is a remarkable and stunning testimony to the power of Jesus' influence and message to reach all people, even beyond those who called themselves Christians. Josephus ends his mention of Christ by saying: "he was perhaps the Messiah concerning whom the prophets have recounted wonders."

There are not many other contemporary mentions of Jesus' life and work, though historians do describe his committed and persecuted disciples. Even so, we can learn a great deal by studying the culture and times in which Jesus lived. Learning about the first-century Roman empire, or about Jewish laws at the time, for instance, can shed new light on the power and insight of Jesus' teachings.

WHILE THE FIRST FOUR BOOKS OF THE NEW TESTAMENT ARE OUR PRIMARY SOURCE FOR INFORMATION ON THE LIFE OF JESUS, THE OLD TESTAMENT CONTAINS PROPHECIES THAT CAN BE INTERPRETED AS FORETELLING THE APPEARANCE OF GOD'S PROMISED MESSIAH, THE SAVIOR WHO WOULD DELIVER THE JEWISH NATION AND THE WHOLE WORLD FROM DESTRUCTION.

CHRISTIAN BELIEVERS POINT TO MANY PROPHECIES IN THE OLD TESTAMENT AS BEING FULFILLED IN JESUS' LIFE, DEATH, AND RESURRECTION; THE NUMBER VARIES FROM AN ESTIMATED THREE HUNDRED TO FIVE HUNDRED. HERE ARE A FEW OF THE MOST FAMILIAR OF THEM.

Old Testament

OLD TESTAMENT CONNECTIONS

THE MESSIAH WOULD BE:	JESUS WAS:
Born of a virgin Isaiah 7:14	Born to Mary Matthew 1:20–23; Luke 2:5–7
A descendant of Abraham Genesis 12:1–3; 22:18	A descendant of Abraham, according to Matthew's genealogy Matthew 1:1–2
A descendant of the tribe of Judah Genesis 49:10	A descendant of Judah, according to Luke's genealogy Luke 3:33
A descendant of David 2 Samuel 7:12–16	A descendant of David, according to Matthew's genealogy Matthew 1:1
Born in Bethlehem Micah 5:2	Born in Bethlehem because of the census Matthew 2:1–6; Luke 2:1–4
Taken to Egypt Hosea 11:1	Taken to Egypt to escape Herod's slaughter of baby boys Matthew 2:13–15
Heralded by a messenger Isaiah 40:3–5; Malachi 3:1	Introduced by John the Baptist Matthew 3:1–3; Mark 1:1–3; Luke 3:1–6; John 1:23–27
Entering Jerusalem on a donkey Zechariah 9:9	Hailed by his disciples as he rode into Jerusalem on a donkey Matthew 21:4–11; John 12:12–15
Betrayed for 30 pieces of silver Zechariah 11:12–13	Betrayed by Judas for thirty pieces of silver Matthew 26:14–16; 27:3–10

Ancient religious mosaic in Rome

t Connections

THE MESSIAH WOULD BE:	JESUS WAS:
Silent before his accusers	Accused falsely in court, but didn't answer
Isaiah 53:7	Matthew 27:11–14; Mark 15:1–5; Luke 23:9
Crucified, with his hands, feet, and side pierced	Crucified, with nails through his hands and feet and his side pierced with a spear
Psalm 22:16; Zechariah 12:10	Matthew 27:35; Mark 15:24–25; Luke 23:33; 24:39; John 19:18; 34–37; 20:20–28
Given gall and vinegar to drink	Offered gall as he hung on the cross
Psalm 69:21	Matthew 27:34; Mark 15:23; Luke 23:36; John 19:29
Pronounced dead with no broken bones	Not subjected to having his legs broken
Exodus 12:46; Numbers 9:12; Psalm 34:20	John 19:31–37
The owner of a garment for which lots were cast	On the cross as the soldiers gambled for his clothes
Psalm 22:18	Matthew 27:35; Mark 15:24; Luke 23:34; John 19:24
Put to death with sinners	Hung on the cross between two thieves
Isaiah 53:8–12	Matthew 27:38; Luke 23:32–33
Buried by a rich man	Buried by Joseph of Arimethea
Isaiah 53:9	Matthew 27:57–60; Mark 15:42–46; Luke 23:50–54; John 19:38–42
Raised from the dead	Raised to life on Sunday morning
Psalm 16:10	Matthew 28:1–6; Mark 16:1–6; Luke 24:1–8; John 20:11–18; Acts 2:31

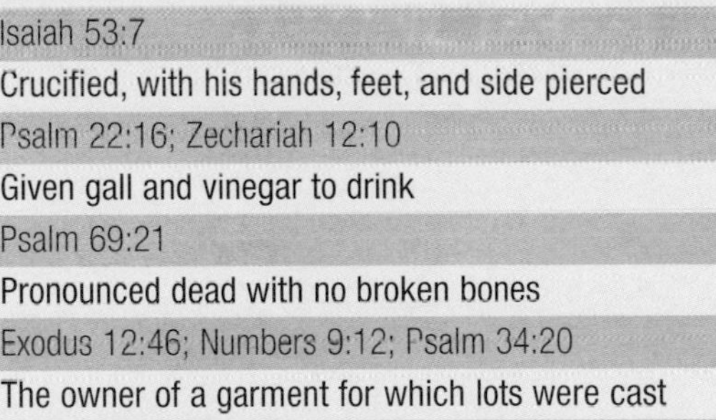

A QUOTE FROM THE BIBLE

LUKE 24:44

Jesus said . . . "Everything written about me in the Law of Moses, the Books of the Prophets, and in the Psalms had to happen."

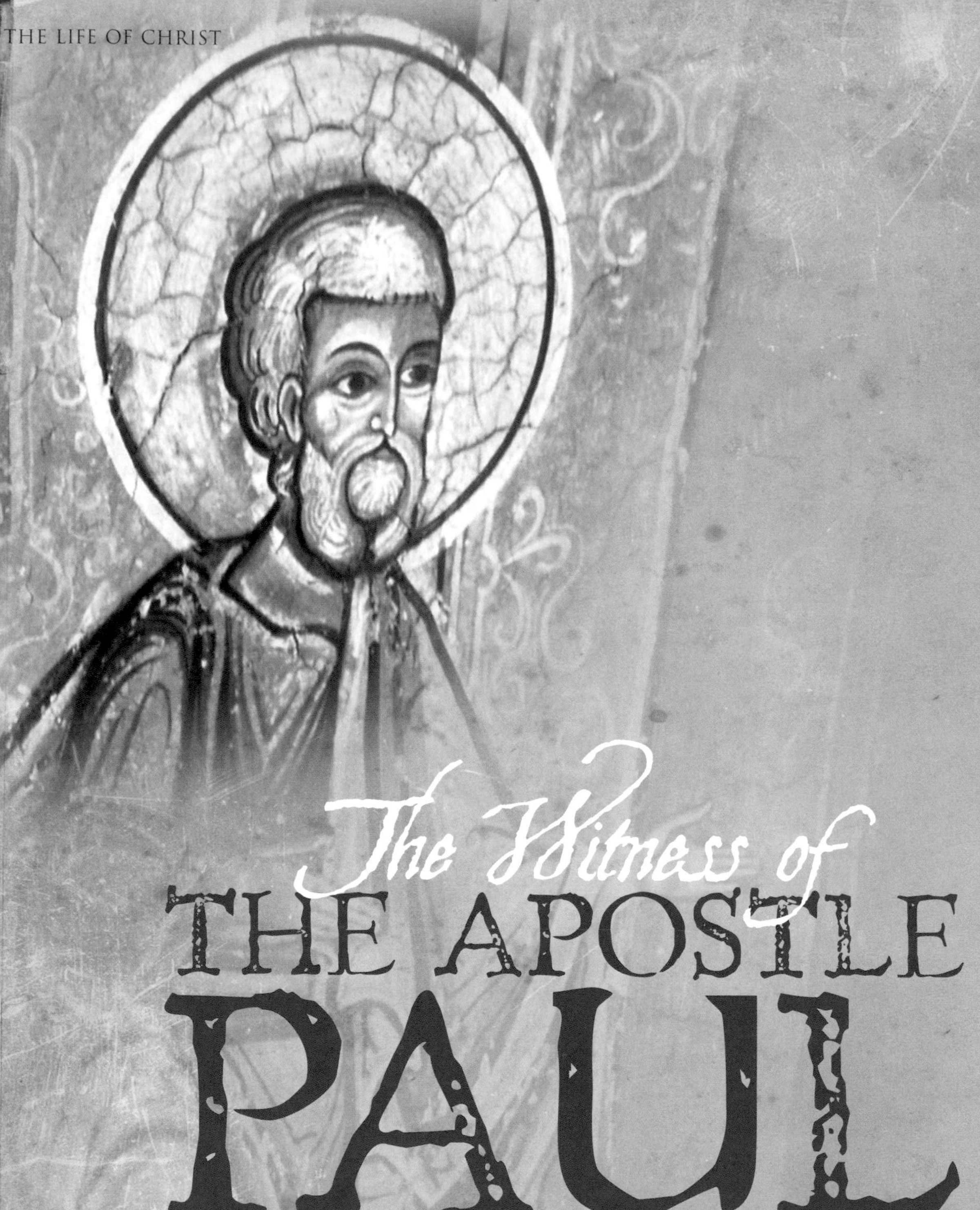

The Witness of THE APOSTLE PAUL

PAUL OF TARSUS, KNOWN THROUGH CHURCH HISTORY AS ST. PAUL, WAS A UNIQUE WITNESS TO JESUS' LIFE AND MINISTRY. ORIGINALLY HOSTILE TO THE FOLLOWERS OF JESUS, PAUL AGGRESSIVELY PERSECUTED CHRISTIANS. WITHIN A FEW SHORT YEARS OF JESUS' DEATH, HOWEVER, PAUL BECAME A DISCIPLE OF JESUS AND SPENT MUCH OF HIS REMAINING LIFE BOLDLY PREACHING THE CHRISTIAN FAITH (SEE ACTS 9:1–31). THE FOLLOWING ARE EXCERPTS FROM TWO OF PAUL'S LETTERS.

Christ is Truly God

ROMANS 1:1–6

FROM PAUL,
A SERVANT OF CHRIST JESUS.

GOD CHOSE ME TO BE AN APOSTLE, AND HE APPOINTED ME TO PREACH THE GOOD NEWS THAT HE PROMISED LONG AGO BY WHAT HIS PROPHETS SAID IN THE HOLY SCRIPTURES. THIS GOOD NEWS IS ABOUT HIS SON, OUR LORD JESUS CHRIST! AS A HUMAN, HE WAS FROM THE FAMILY OF DAVID. BUT THE HOLY SPIRIT PROVED THAT JESUS IS THE POWERFUL SON OF GOD, BECAUSE HE WAS RAISED FROM DEATH.

JESUS WAS KIND TO ME AND CHOSE ME TO BE AN APOSTLE, SO THAT PEOPLE OF ALL NATIONS WOULD OBEY AND HAVE FAITH.

A QUOTE FROM THE BIBLE

PHILIPPIANS 2:6–8

Christ was truly God.
But he did not try to remain
equal with God.
Instead he gave up everything and
became a slave,
when he became
like one of us.
Christ was humble.
He obeyed God
and even died
on a cross.
Then God gave Christ
the highest place
and honored his name
above all others.
So at the name of Jesus
everyone will bow down,
those in heaven, on earth,
and under the earth.
And to the glory
of God the Father
everyone will openly agree,
"Jesus Christ is Lord!"

Jesus' Birth and Childhood

The birth of the Christ child is celebrated in myriad ways throughout our culture. The familiar story is recreated on church lawns and chapel ceilings, in frescos and in stained glass. Images of the nativity occupy retail shelves and adorn greeting cards by the truckload.

We observe the birthday of Jesus as a joyous annual festival, the centerpiece of our winter holidays. Yet this sacred event has become so mingled and intertwined with secular contemporary culture that we often have to take a step back to regain our perspective and remember what we are really observing: the simple story of Mary, Joseph, and a newborn baby adored by shepherds and mystical wise men.

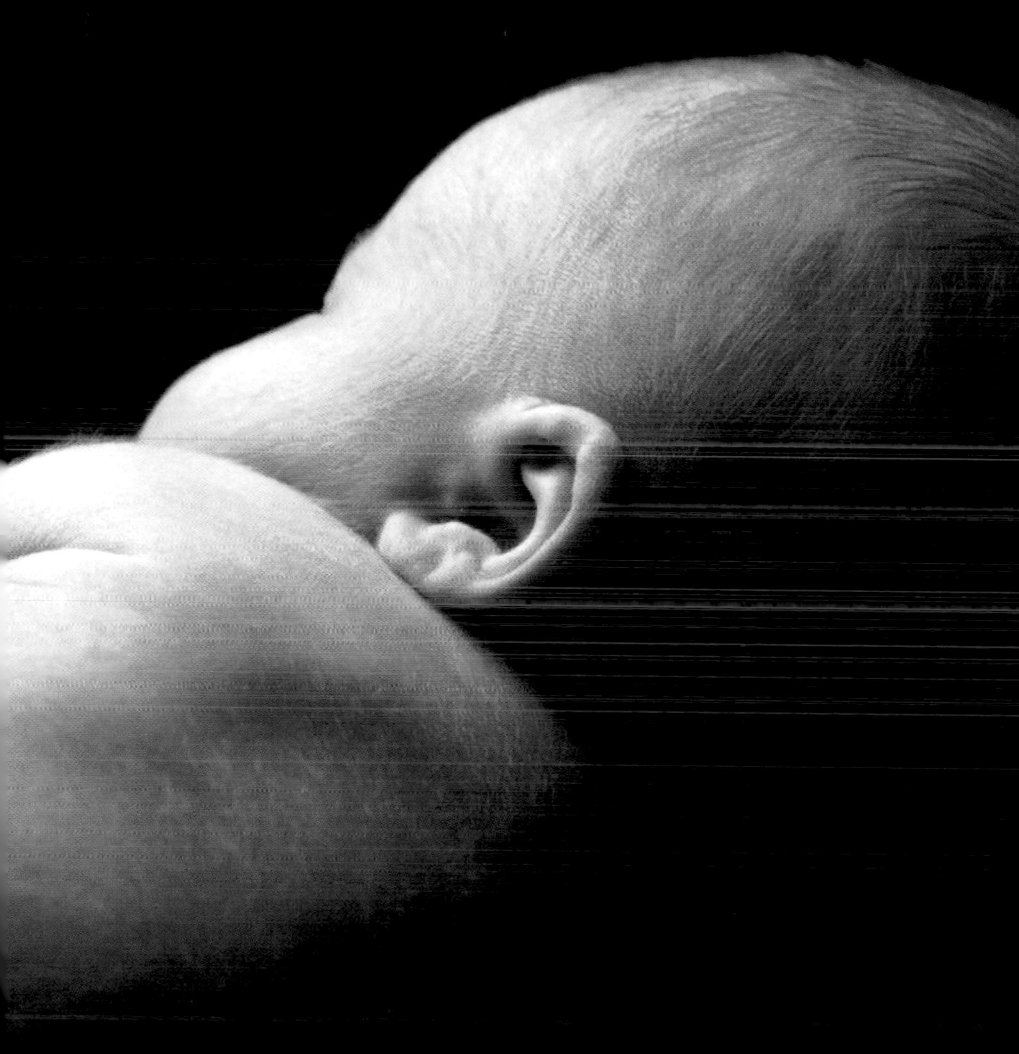

The tale of Jesus' birth is both sublime and humble. It soars with the ethereal sound of angels singing in chorus, then comes down to earth to deal with the practical concerns of fashioning a baby's bed from a feeding trough in a lowly manger.

That God would choose to become one with humanity in all our vulnerability, humbling himself to experience life with us, is a challenging idea. Its enormity is hard to capture fully in a children's nativity pageant or in the words of an old Christmas carol. It is in the private heart of each of us that we must accept these good tidings of great joy: that God became man to live and die and live again, reaching out

to share the experience of his creation, humanity, and to draw us closer to himself.

The pages that follow present the facts we know from scripture about the birth of Christ, who is also called Immanuel, which means "God with us."

The Story of Jesus' Birth

A HUMBLE BEGINNING

Weaving together Matthew's and Luke's accounts, we are able to reconstruct the events surrounding Jesus' birth.

It began unlike any pregnancy before or since. An angel appeared to a young Jewish girl, Mary, who was probably only twelve- to fourteen-years old, and delivered a stunning message: she would give birth to a son, who was the Son of God. Though an engagement had already been arranged for Mary, she was not yet married, and an unplanned pregnancy in her society at that historical moment would brand her with shame. Would anyone believe that the child in her womb had been conceived by the Holy Spirit? Who in their right mind would believe this young girl to be anything but delusional when she announced she was destined to give birth to God's Son?

Certainly the man with the most to lose was her fiancé, Joseph. The carpenter planned a quiet divorce to shame the young woman as little as possible. But his fears were quieted when an angel also appeared in his dreams, reiterating Mary's claims: This child, the Son of God, was to be named Jesus, which means "the Lord saves" (Matthew 1:21). Joseph believed the vision and he and Mary were married.

As Mary's due date approached, the young couple had to undertake an overland journey from Nazareth to Bethlehem, a distance of around 65 miles. The Romans, who had some level of control over the region for more than two hundred years, had called a census of the entire imperial province of Judea. Families were to return to their hometowns (or at least the hometown of the head of the family) in order to be counted. Since the Judeans were exempt from Roman military service, this census was most likely for taxation purposes.

The great influx of people assembling for the census swelled the streets. Lodging houses had filled rapidly, and Joseph and Mary couldn't find a room of their own for the night. Nature couldn't wait: when the birth pains began, Mary had the baby right where they had taken shelter—nearby, perhaps even in an animal stall. She laid her newborn son in the bed most obviously available, the feeding trough for the animals.

While Joseph was thinking about this, an angel from the Lord appeared to him in a dream. The angel said, "Joseph, the baby that Mary will have is from the Holy Spirit. Go ahead and marry her. Then after her baby is born, name him Jesus, because he will save his people from their sins." Matthew. 1:20–21

At that moment, just outside Bethlehem, a group of unsuspecting shepherds tended their flocks beneath a starry sky. Suddenly, piercing the darkness with radiant light, an angel appeared in front of them, scaring them witless. But the angel calmed them with an announcement of great joy: a Savior had been born in Jerusalem, King David's hometown (Luke 2:10–11). (David was one of Israel's most beloved early kings, a visionary and poet, and many of the psalms in the Old Testament are attributed to him.)

Mary and Infant Jesus.
Ancient Russian Icon

Adoration of the Magi.
Mosaic.
Cavallini, Pietro (c.1250–1330)
Location: S. Maria in Trastevere, Rome, Italy

As the shepherds watched in wonder, the heavens suddenly filled with countless angels, worshiping and praising God. The astounded shepherds abandoned their watch to find this Savior proclaimed by the angel. Once they found him, they shared their fantastic story with everyone they encountered.

Others bore witness to the divine birth. From far beyond the borders of Judea, scholars and men of wisdom, known to their culture as magi, saw a bright star in the nighttime sky that signified the birth of a great ruler. They traveled tirelessly on to the city of Jerusalem, where they inquired of the Roman ruler, Herod, where they might find the new baby king in order to worship him and pay their respects with the priceless gifts they had carried with them for that purpose.

But the kingdom of this newborn child was not of this world. Jesus' destiny was not to rule politically, though many in his time never understood that. Herod was one of them: when he heard the magi's description, he perceived the newborn "king" as a threat to his throne. Making an effort to mask his jealousy, even as he was hatching dark schemes to have his infant rival killed, Herod asked the wise men to return to him after they found the king, asserting that he, too, might worship him.

When the wise men finally did find Jesus playing at Mary's feet, perhaps as much as two years after his birth, the foreign travelers fell to the ground in praise and lavished their gifts—gold, frankincense, and myrrh—upon the child. The number of gifts has frequently led to the assumption that there were three wise men in all, but the Bible does not give their names.

Having fulfilled their hearts' desire—to behold with their own eyes the great king whose birth the star heralded—God warned these Eastern travelers not to return to Herod, but instead to slip silently from his kingdom. Joseph, too, received a warning in a dream to take his family to Egypt until they were safe from Herod (Matthew 2:13). In this way, Jesus escaped Herod's wrath, for the frightened ruler, fearful of losing this throne, now ordered a massacre: every male child two years and younger in the region of Bethlehem was killed.

The Importance of Christ's Genealogy

The four Gospels that tell us of the life of Christ are very different, and each recounts the story in its own way. Mark begins his tale with the herald of God, John the Baptist, proclaiming Jesus' identity. Luke's story begins even earlier, with the announcement of John the Baptist's birth 30 years before the public ministry of Jesus. John's Gospel tells the story from the very beginning of history, opening with the words "In the beginning was the one who is called the Word" (John 1:1).

Matthew begins his tale in the midst of Jewish history (1:1–17), placing Jesus firmly in the genealogical context of the Jewish people, suggesting his heritage was a harbinger of his divinity. His ancestor Enoch was known for walking closely with God (Genesis 5:24). Rahab, a woman outside the Israelite community and a prostitute as well, entered into the lineage of Christ because she had faith in the God of the Israelites and assisted Israel's army in the famous battle of Jericho.

An even more renowned ancestor of Jesus was King David, whom the Bible calls a man who pleased God (Acts 13:22). None of these human ancestors lived flawless lives, but in their strengths and weaknesses, God's will was working to bring his Son into human history.

THIS IS HOW JESUS CHRIST WAS BORN. A YOUNG WOMAN NAMED MARY WAS ENGAGED TO JOSEPH FROM KING DAVID'S FAMILY. BUT BEFORE THEY WERE MARRIED, SHE LEARNED THAT SHE WAS GOING TO HAVE A BABY BY GOD'S HOLY SPIRIT. JOSEPH WAS A GOOD MAN AND DID NOT WANT TO EMBARRASS MARY IN FRONT OF EVERYONE. SO HE DECIDED TO QUIETLY CALL OFF THE WEDDING.

WHILE JOSEPH WAS THINKING ABOUT THIS, AN ANGEL FROM THE LORD APPEARED TO HIM IN A DREAM. THE ANGEL SAID, "JOSEPH, THE BABY THAT MARY WILL HAVE IS FROM THE HOLY SPIRIT. GO AHEAD AND MARRY HER. THEN AFTER HER BABY IS BORN, NAME HIM JESUS, BECAUSE HE WILL SAVE HIS PEOPLE FROM THEIR SINS."

SO THE LORD'S PROMISE CAME TRUE, JUST AS THE PROPHET HAD SAID, "A VIRGIN WILL HAVE A BABY BOY, AND HE WILL BE CALLED IMMANUEL," WHICH MEANS "GOD IS WITH US."

AFTER JOSEPH WOKE UP, HE AND MARY WERE SOON MARRIED, JUST AS THE LORD'S ANGEL HAD TOLD HIM TO DO.

MATTHEW 1:18–24

Jesus Grows Up

"WHO HAS BELIEVED OUR MESSAGE AND TO WHOM HAS THE ARM OF THE LORD BEEN REVEALED? HE GREW UP BEFORE HIM LIKE A TENDER SHOOT, AND LIKE A ROOT OUT OF DRY GROUND."

The New Testament paints its portrait of Jesus' childhood with very few strokes, but the Gospels according to Matthew and Luke do provide a few details of his growing years. Luke summarizes the life of the young Jesus by simply saying that he grew in height and in wisdom just like the other boys of his day (Luke 2:40).

Jesus at Two

According to Matthew's Gospel (2:13–23), while Jesus was still a baby, God warned Joseph in a dream of King Herod's murderous intention: to rid the land of any possible rival to his throne. The Old Testament had promised the Jewish people that a Messiah would come to save them. While expectations for a future deliverer were prevalent, some hoped for a military king like David, who would defeat their oppressors (e.g., the Roman authorities), and others hoped for a prophet like Moses a messianic figure chosen by God to bring salvation and speak God's word. Mary and Joseph fled to Egypt with their newborn son and escaped the bloodbath that Herod rained upon every male child in Jerusalem who was two or under.

Jesus at Twelve

Joseph and Mary probably traveled to Jerusalem every year to celebrate the ancient Jewish feast of Passover. Jerusalem was the center of Jewish worship, so for this, the most significant religious feast, as many Jewish families as were able would caravan together for a time of celebration and worship. Jesus would logically have accompanied his family on the journey.

On their return to Galilee in the year Jesus was twelve, his parents traveled an entire day before realizing their son was not with their party. Strange as this may sound to our ears, in that day large groups of extended family and friends traveled together, and Jesus' parents probably assumed he was in the company of relatives or friends.

Frantic, Jesus' parents rushed back to Jerusalem and spent three agonizing days searching for their missing son. They finally found Jesus at the city's main temple, where the priests had welcomed him more as a peer in spiritual matters than as a young boy. When Joseph and Mary understandably chided him for wandering off, their gifted son asked them why they hadn't thought to look for him in the temple—his Father's house (Luke 2:42–50). This is one of the earliest manifestations of his divine nature.

The 12-year-old Jesus in the Temple.
Oil on canvas. 1879.
Liebermann, Max (1847–1935)
Location: Hamburger Kunsthalle, Hamburg, Germany

A QUOTE FROM THE BIBLE

LUKE 2:41–51

Every year Jesus' parents went to Jerusalem for Passover. And when Jesus was twelve years old, they all went there as usual for the celebration. After Passover his parents left, but they did not know that Jesus had stayed on in the city...
Three days later they found Jesus sitting in the temple, listening to the teachers and asking them questions...
His mother kept on thinking about all that had happened.

Traditions and Legends

Where history leaves gaps, traditions and legends often rush to fill in the details. Here are a few examples of the traditions and legends that have arisen around the story of the Christ-child.

Many people have tried to tell the story of what God has done among us. They wrote what we had been told by the ones who were there in the beginning and saw what happened. So I made a careful study of everything and then decided to write and tell you exactly what took place. Honorable Theophilus, I have done this to let you know the truth about what you have heard. Luke 1:1–4

Jesus was born near the beginning of the first century AD.

Matthew set his Gospel account of Jesus' birth in historical context, during the reign of Herod the King (Herod the Great ruled Judea from 37 BC – 4 BC). Because we know the date of Herod's death, a key event in this story, we have a firm time marker, one that is somewhat surprising. If Jesus was born while Herod was still ruling, then Jesus was born before 4 BC.

Young Jesus learned miracles from Egyptian magicians.

According to Matthew's Gospel (2:13–23), Joseph fled to Egypt with Mary and Jesus to escape Herod's killing of all baby boys in the region. After Herod died, they returned to Nazareth. Jesus would have been two years old at the time. He would have been far too young to interact with the Egyptian mystics.

The child Jesus made clay pigeons come to life.

Apocryphal Gospels tell of the child Jesus performing miracles flourished during the centuries immediately following his death and resurrection. But John records Jesus' miracle of turning water into wine at the wedding at Cana as his first (John 2:11). Though Jesus could have performed miracles as a child, the New Testament offers no credible evidence to support that idea.

Young Jesus raised friends from the dead

The Infancy Gospels are apocryphal. These are texts that purport to record historic events, but are not accepted as authentic biblical scripture. *The Infancy Gospel of Thomas* describes numerous miracles, including one in which Jesus resurrects a friend who had died after falling from a roof.

MIRACLES

THE POWER OF JESUS CHRIST

Jesus' miracles were a remarkable element of his ministry, but their significance cut both ways, for the wonders he worked were sometimes misinterpreted. The miracles—his power over sickness, his mastery of nature, his banishing of evil, even his authority over death—served to reveal Jesus' power as the Son of God. Yet at times they also left the people simply clamoring for more astonishments rather than nourishing a growing faith. The shouting for wonders could drown out Christ's revolutionary message of love and salvation.

Thus, when required to produce a sign of his power, Jesus often refused. Instead, he countered with his own demand, asking that his followers and accusers demonstrate more faith and less interest in miracles.

The Gospels are replete with accounts of Jesus healing the sick and even bringing the dead back to life. Blind men regained their sight. Diseases disappeared. And there were times when Jesus didn't even have to be in a room or even in the same house to perform a miracle. He merely spoke the word, responding to the faith of those who asked for the healing.

Some of Jesus' miracles demonstrated his power over the natural world. He walked on water. He calmed storms at sea. He broke bread and it was transformed into multiple loaves.

Jesus also miraculously defeated supernatural evil. He forced demons from people's bodies. He faced down Satan himself. He was recognized on more than one occasion by demonic forces, even when the people surrounding him remained unaware of his divine identity.

The story of the life of Christ is incomplete without the miraculous. While his ministry involved much more than just signs and wonders, it was marked by demonstrations of supernatural ability, events that lead us to a great question: what kind of person could possess such powers?

the LIFE OF CHRIST
CHAPTER
5
miracles

HEALINGS

JESUS' POWER OVER SICKNESS

The writer of the Gospel according to John ends his eyewitness account of Jesus' life by saying that if every one of the things Jesus did were written down, "I don't suppose there would be room enough in the whole world for all the books" (John 21:25).

There's no way of knowing how many lives were changed by the healing touch—and the healing words—of Jesus. But the three encounters recorded below reveal Jesus' compassion for the sick and disabled, as well as his power over their natural afflictions.

The Centurion's Servant

In Capernaum, a city in Galilee, Jesus met a Roman centurion. The centurion was a Gentile, a man who knew nothing about the Messiah or other biblical prophecies. What the centurion did understand was authority: as a soldier, he was trained to recognize superior power and respond to it properly.

Perhaps that training helped him see something incredible in Jesus: a power that was not of this world. The centurion realized that in the universal chain of command, physical afflictions and sickness somehow fell under the authority of the seemingly nondescript man standing in front of him. Indeed, the centurion believed that one command from Jesus would be sufficient to heal one of his servants who was ailing. And he was right (Matthew 8:5–13).

Confessing his unworthiness, the Roman asked if Jesus could simply bless his ailing servant. Then Jesus said to the officer, "You may go home now. Your faith has made it happen." At that moment, his servant was healed (Matthew 8:13).

Christ heals a blind man.
Relief (3rd CE) on an early Christian sarcophagus from Mezzocamino, Via Ostiense, Rome. Cat. 41. Location: Museo Nazionale Romano (Terme di Diocleziano), Museo Nazionale Romano, Rome, Italy

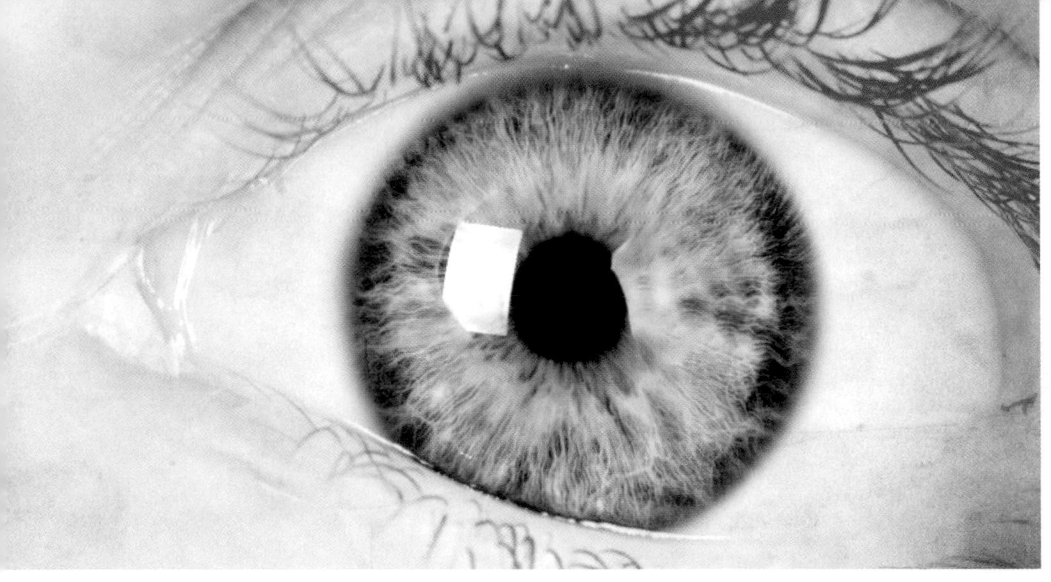

As Jesus walked along, he saw a man who had been blind since birth... "Because of his blindness, you will see God work a miracle for him."
John 9:1–3

The Woman Who Bled

Twelve years. That's how long one woman had suffered from her bleeding. Doctors tried, but they could do nothing for her. She had one last hope: the man called Jesus. Stories of the miracle-worker's healing powers had spread throughout Jerusalem. Crowds had begun following him everywhere, begging for healing.

And now here he was, just a few feet away from her. But the jostling throng prevented her from getting any closer, and she watched in horror as her last chance for health passed her by. In desperation, she reached out and touched the edge of Jesus' cloak. It was a single, glancing touch, yet that one touch was enough: the woman was instantly healed.

Jesus turned around and asked who had touched him. The woman, now frightened, fell at his feet and explained her situation (Luke 8:43–48).

In response, she heard these words: "You are now well because of your faith. May God give you peace!" (Luke 8:48).

Miracles: Religious Leaders Demanded Them . . .

The Pharisees came out and started an argument with Jesus. They wanted to test him by asking for a sign from heaven. Jesus groaned and said, "Why are you always looking for a sign? I can promise you that you will not be given one!" Then he left them. He again got into a boat and crossed over to the other side of the lake.
(Mark 8:11–13)

The Man Born Blind

A popular notion among Jewish religious leaders in Jesus' day, and one that persists even today in some cultures, was that a person's sickness or disability was God's punishment for some sin committed by a person or a person's family members. As a result, sick and disabled people were often shunned and even vilified by the public.

As Jesus was walking with his disciples in Jerusalem one day, he saw a man who had been born blind. His disciples asked him who was to blame for the man's condition. Jesus assured them that neither the man nor his parents had caused his blindness. And he proceeded to show them that even the most tragic situations have the potential to bring glory to God.

Jesus spit in the dirt and rubbed mud over the blind man's eyes. He then instructed the man to wash himself in the nearby Pool of Siloam. The man did as he was instructed. And when he emerged from the pool, his vision had been restored, and he was able to see for the first time in his life (John 9:1–7).

CREATION

JESUS' POWER OVER NATURE

Through many miracles, Jesus demonstrated supernatural power, which seemed to bend the rules of nature. As the creator of everything, Jesus held power over it all: "Everything was created by him, everything in heaven and on earth, everything seen and unseen, including all forces and powers . . . All things were created by God's Son, and everything was made for him." (Colossians 1:16)

Calming the Storm

The Sea of Galilee was known for its sudden, violent storms. Jesus and his disciples encountered such a storm one day as they sailed from Galilee to Gerasa. Jesus was asleep when the squall broke—a storm violent enough to frighten even the experienced fishermen on the boat.

As wave after enormous wave threatened to capsize the vessel, the panicked disciples awakened Jesus. What they expected him to do is unclear, but it's safe to say none of them expected him to speak to the wind and waves. Yet that's just what he did, commanding the elements to be still.

Immediately the wind ceased and the water became smooth as glass. Yet the disciples remained uneasy. They looked at the One they had been following in a new light. "Who is this?" they asked themselves. "Even the wind and the waves obey him!" (Mark 4:35–41).

That same expression of awe—and the slowly dawning realization that only God himself can supersede his creation—can be found in other accounts of Jesus' power over nature.

The Miracle of Christ Turning the Water Into Wine at the Marriage at Cana.
Early Christian mosaic. 6th CE.
Location: S. Apollinare Nuovo, Ravenna, Italy

The best wine is always served first. Then after the guests have had plenty, the other wine is served. But you have kept the best until last!
John 2:9

Turning Water into Wine

According to John's Gospel, Jesus' first recorded miracle occurred during a wedding in Cana. A guest at the wedding, Jesus was pulled aside by his mother, who explained that the host had run out of wine. In Jewish culture at that time, such an oversight would have been a humiliating social faux pas.

Jesus instructed the host's servants to fill six stone jars with water and then draw some water out and take it to the host. The host took a sip, but the liquid in the jar had been transformed; he tasted excellent wine instead of water. He remarked on the superior quality of the wine since it was the normal custom for the best wine to be served first, but here the best wine was offered later in the celebration (John 2:1–11).

Cursing a Fig Tree

Jesus did not do miracles in order to entertain his audience, but to teach them. He intended that every miracle illustrate the spiritual and moral lessons he was teaching. On a certain occasion, Jesus had a conflict with the religious leaders of the day. Rather than providing people with spiritual nourishment and shelter, Jesus confronted their greed and hypocrisy. The next morning, he illustrated the value of these teachers when he approached a fig tree with his disciples. After failing to find any fruit on the tree, Jesus cursed the tree, which instantly withered. The useless tree became an illustration of these worthless leaders (Matthew 21:12–27).

Miracles: Townspeople Disbelieved Them . . .

Jesus went to his hometown. He taught in its synagogue, and the people were so amazed that they asked, "Where does he get all this wisdom and the power to work these miracles? Isn't he the son of the carpenter? Isn't Mary his mother, and aren't James, Joseph, Simon, and Judas his brothers? Don't his sisters still live here in our town? How can he do all this?" So the people were upset because of what he was doing.

But Jesus said, "Prophets are honored by everyone, except the people of their hometown and their own family." And because the people did not have any faith, Jesus did not work many miracles there.
(Matthew 13:54–58)

WALKING ON WATER

JESUS' POWER OVER NATURE

The setting was the Sea of Galilee. The conditions were brutal, and it was the middle of the night. Jesus' disciples, their boat bobbing up and down in the waves, were struggling to make headway against a fierce wind when they saw an amazing and disturbing sight. Something, or someone, was coming toward them . . . walking on the water.

At first the suspicious men thought the figure was a ghost— perhaps some kind of water spirit—which, according to Jewish superstition, was a portent of disaster. But as the figure grew closer, they recognized Jesus, in the flesh, demonstrating that the laws of physics did not apply to him as he strode without fear across the waves (Matthew 14:22–33). Read the story on the next page.

MATTHEW 14:22-33

At once, Jesus made his disciples get into a boat and start back across the lake. But he stayed until he had sent the crowds away. Then he went up on a mountain where he could be alone and pray. Later that evening, he was still there. By this time the boat was a long way from the shore. It was going against the wind and was being tossed around by the waves. A little while before morning, Jesus came walking on the water toward his disciples. When they saw him, they thought he was a ghost. They were terrified and started screaming.

At once, Jesus said to them, "Don't worry! I am Jesus. Don't be afraid."

Peter replied, "Lord, if it is really you, tell me to come to you on the water."

"Come on!" Jesus said. Peter then got out of the boat and started walking on the water toward him.

But when Peter saw how strong the wind was, he was afraid and started sinking. "Save me, Lord!" he shouted.

At once, Jesus reached out his hand. He helped Peter up and said, "You surely don't have much faith. Why do you doubt?"

When Jesus and Peter got into the boat, the wind died down. The men in the boat worshiped Jesus and said, "You really are the Son of God!"

FEEDING FIVE THOUSAND

AFTER JOHN THE BAPTIST WAS EXECUTED, JESUS RETREATED TO A REMOTE PLACE FOR SOME TIME ALONE. HOWEVER, WHEN WORD SPREAD OF THE CHARISMATIC PREACHER'S RETREAT, PEOPLE FOLLOWED HIM. THE BIBLE PUTS THE NUMBER OF THE FOLLOWERS AT FIVE THOUSAND. (SOME SCHOLARS POINT OUT THAT OFTEN ONLY MEN WERE COUNTED IN SUCH SITUATIONS, AND THAT WHEN YOU ADD WOMEN AND CHILDREN TO THE TALLY, THE TOTAL NUMBER WAS LIKELY EVEN HIGHER.)

THE PEOPLE HAD COME FOR HEALING, AND JESUS OBLIGED THEM. AS THE HOUR GREW LATE, THOUGH, THE LARGE CROWD BECAME HUNGRY. NO ONE, IT SEEMS, HAD BROUGHT FOOD ALONG, SAVE FOR ONE BOY WHO HAD FIVE SMALL BARLEY LOAVES AND TWO FISH.

JESUS TOOK THE BOY'S MEAGER PROVISIONS, OFFERED A PRAYER OF THANKS, AND BEGAN TO DISTRIBUTE THE BREAD AND FISH TO HIS DISCIPLES. THE DISCIPLES, IN TURN, HANDED IT OUT TO THE CROWD.

FIVE LOAVES AND TWO FISH: IT SHOULD HAVE PROVIDED ONLY A QUICK BITE FOR A LUCKY FEW—BUT SOMETHING AMAZING HAPPENED. NO MATTER HOW MANY PEOPLE HE SERVED, JESUS NEVER RAN OUT OF BREAD OR FISH. AS HIS DISCIPLES PASSED THROUGH THE CROWD, SHARING THE FOOD, EVERYONE ATE UNTIL HE OR SHE WAS FULL. AND WHEN THE MEAL WAS DONE, THE DISCIPLES COLLECTED TWELVE BASKETFULS OF LEFTOVERS. (READ THE FULL STORY IN JOHN 6:1–13)

A QUOTE FROM THE BIBLE

JOHN 6:9–11

"There is a boy here who has five small loaves of barley bread and two fish. But what good is that with all these people?" The ground was covered with grass, and Jesus told his disciples to have everyone sit down. About five thousand men were in the crowd. Jesus took the bread in his hands and gave thanks to God. Then he passed the bread to the people, and he did the same with the fish, until everyone had plenty to eat.

EXORCISMS

JESUS' POWER OVER EVIL

The New Testament records many accounts of demonic possession, in which demons attacked people internally, operating from within their spirit. It also records incidents in which evil spirits victimized people externally, attacking them from outside. Here are some examples of demonic possession:

- A who woman was afflicted by a demon for 18 years, differentiating her from others who had battled long-term illnesses (Luke 13:11).
- Mary Magdalene, a woman from whom Jesus cast out seven demons (Luke 8:2)
- A mute man (Matthew 9:32–33), and a blind and mute man (Matthew 12:22)
- A little boy (Luke 9:37–43a)
- A man in the synagogue (Mark 1:23–26)

In each of these cases, Jesus overpowered and cast out the evil spirits who were afflicting the victims. The common denominator of these accounts can be found in the story of one such encounter near the Sea of Galilee.

In the little village of Gerasa, in the Gentile region of the Decapolis, a terror dwelled. Hidden among the tombs of a roadside cemetery was a demoniac—a man possessed by evil spirits. Unsuspecting travelers who ventured too close risked his violent attack.

Jesus Casting Devils Out of a Kneeling Man, c1890.
Tissot, James Jacques Joseph (1836–1902)
Location: Ann Ronan Picture Library, London, Great Britain

Go home to your family and tell them how much the Lord has done for you, and how he has had mercy on you.
Mark 5:19

The people of Gerasa did their best to protect themselves. They tried binding the man's hands and feet with iron chains, but he was strong enough to break the chains. They posted guards to watch over him, but he eluded them. Night and day they heard his horrific cries and waited, shivering in fear, for a possible assault.

The demoniac presented even bigger problems for Jewish travelers in the area. In addition to physical harm, they faced threats to their religious and social standing from this unfortunate man. Jewish law forbade contact with the dead—yet the demoniac chose to dwell in the place of the dead, a cemetery. Thus, those who came into contact with him—even those who survived his assault—could be considered ceremonially unclean.

As Jesus' boat approached the Gerasene shore, however, the demons inside the man immediately recognized him as one who could not be victimized, either by their power or by fears of becoming a cultural outcast.

"'Jesus, Son of God Most High, what do you want with me? I beg you not to torture me!' the demoniac screamed" (Luke 8:28). The encounter that followed was too one-sided to be called a battle. The demons inside the man recognized they were at Jesus' mercy. They begged the miracle-worker to send them into a nearby herd of pigs.

With a single word—"Go!"—Jesus released the man from the control of his evil tormentors. The demons raced out of the man's body and into the pigs, immediately sending the entire herd into the sea, where they drowned (Mark 5:1–20 and Luke 8:26–39).

How did Jesus fight against evil?

Christ used a variety of methods to demonstrate his power over the forces of darkness. Here are some of the ways Jesus overcame demons:

1. By simply speaking to the demons, and by instructing his followers to speak to them in his name (Matthew 8:16; Mark 1:25; 9:25;16:17)
2. By summoning the power of the Holy Spirit (Matthew 12:28; Acts 10:38)
3. By restraining the demons' influence and actions, which the Gospels speak of as binding or tying up the demon (Matthew 12:29; Mark 3:27)
4. Through the power of prayer (Mark 9:28, 29)
5. Through knowing and quoting scripture (Luke 4:1–13)

RESURRECTIONS

JESUS' POWER OVER DEATH

People who demonstrate seemingly miraculous power over sickness are not unknown in history. Over the centuries, countless shamans, witch doctors, and naturalists have claimed healing abilities that resemble the miracles the Bible attributes to Jesus.

Furthermore, some of the stories of healing sprinkled throughout the Gospels could be explained rationally by modern medicine: they might be the result of psychosomatic afflictions, or of the power of suggestion, or simply of the human body's amazing ability to heal.

Accounts of Jesus' power over death itself, however, move the discussion into another realm—quite literally. Modern science stands mute in the face of three incidents recorded in the Bible in which Jesus demonstrated his authority over the grave.

The Widow's Son

In the town of Nain, Jesus and his followers encountered a funeral procession for a young man. The mourners carried his body in an open coffin, according to Jewish tradition. When Jesus saw the young man's grieving, widowed mother, his heart went out to her.

Christ interrupted the procession long enough to touch the coffin and say, "Young man, get up!" The mourners were awestruck when the dead man sat up and began to talk. They gave praise to God for caring for his people. (Luke 7:11–17)

Resurrection of Lazarus.
Luca di Tomme (1330–after 1389)
Location: Pinacoteca, Vatican Museums, Vatican State

After the stone had been rolled aside, Jesus looked up toward heaven and prayed, "Father, I thank you for answering my prayer. I know that you always answer my prayers."
John 11:41–42

Jairus's Daughter

On another occasion, a synagogue official named Jairus approached Jesus and begged him to heal his only daughter, who was critically ill. Jesus heard the man's pleas and set off with him to his house. A messenger met them on the way. He told Jairus his daughter was dead and advised him not to bother Jesus anymore.

The news did not deter Jesus, though. He continued to the house, where he was met by wailing mourners. "The child isn't dead," Jesus said. "She is just asleep."

The mourners laughed bitterly. The girl was dead, they knew; they had seen her lifeless body. Their laughter continued when Jesus took the girl's hand and commanded, "Child, get up!" But when the dead girl stood up, the laughter turned to astonishment: what sort of man could bring the dead to life? (Luke 8:40–42, 49–56)

Lazarus

Once Jesus received word from the town of Bethany that his friend Lazarus was sick. Mary and Martha, Lazarus's sisters and two of Jesus' loyal followers, begged the Lord to come to Bethany to heal their brother. This story is recorded in John 11:1–44.

Though he recognized the urgency of their pleas, Jesus could not make the journey for two days. By the time he finally reached Bethany, it was too late: Lazarus was dead.

Martha's words of greeting to the Lord reflect equal parts belief and frustration: "Lord, if you had been here, my brother would not have died." Other mourners echoed her sentiments, revealing the limited scope of their faith. They had no trouble acknowledging Jesus' power over sickness, but the notion that he might have power over death apparently never occurred to them.

So the bereaved crowd objected when Jesus told them to remove the stone from the mouth of the cave where Lazarus's body lay. The act seemed a violation, an insult to the dead man—and the stench of a body that had been decomposing for four days was something no one wanted to smell.

Yet Jesus insisted. When the tomb was opened, he called, "Lazarus, come out!" And a miracle took shape: from the depths of the tomb, Lazarus emerged, still wrapped in his grave clothes, a dead man walking—as alive as the friends and relatives who gazed at him in awe.

Miracles: The Disciples Continued Them…

After the Lord Jesus had said these things to the disciples, he was taken back up to heaven where he sat down at the right side of God. Then the disciples left and preached everywhere. The Lord was with them, and the miracles they worked proved that their message was true. (Mark 16:19–20)

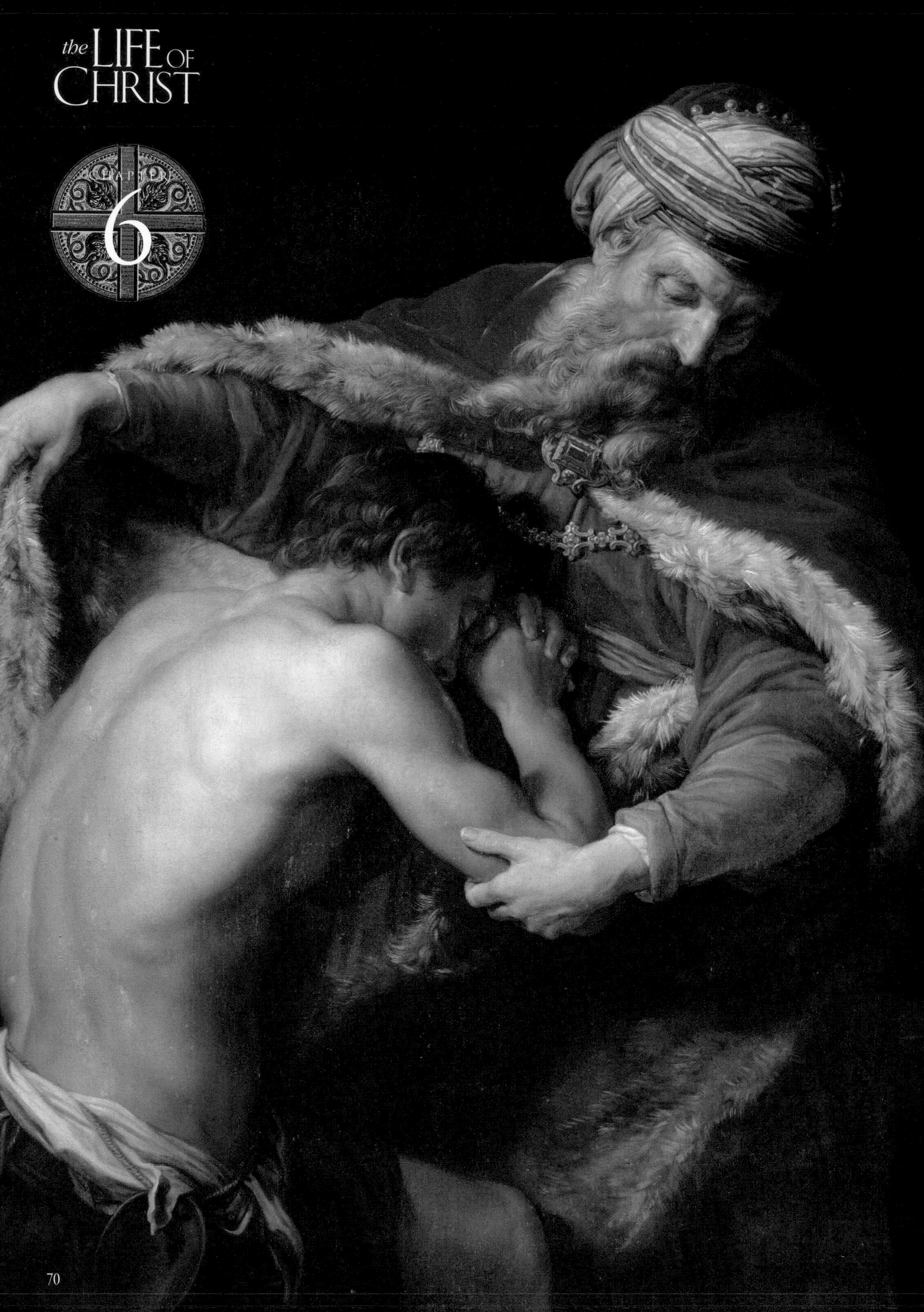
the LIFE OF CHRIST
CHAPTER
6

FAMOUS *Sayings* OF JESUS

Jesus' words of wisdom are woven into our everyday lexicon; they are so much a part of our cultural heritage that we don't always recognize them. It was Jesus who originated phrases like "the faith to move mountains," when he was using an object lesson to teach his disciples.

The scriptural passage known as John 3:16 is perhaps Jesus' most famous saying. It is recorded as part of a conversation he had with a religious leader who came to visit him in secret, since some Jewish religious leaders opposed Jesus. This man, Nicodemus, wanted Jesus' own explanation of what it meant to be a part of the kingdom of God. Jesus told him that God loved the people of this world so much that he gave his only Son to redeem them, so that everyone who has faith in him will have eternal life and will never die spiritually (John 3:16).

Jesus' words, as recorded in the four Gospels, have moved generations. They have been quoted by authors in every age and in every literary form, from the plays of William Shakespeare to the novels of Ernest Hemingway to the poems of Doctor Seuss. The sayings in this chapter are some of the most popular quotes taken from Jesus' teachings, prayers, and parables, explored in their original context. Each of them resonates with the principal themes of his ministry and life: they speak of God's unconditional love, of the forgiving grace he bestows on us, and of the splendor of God's kingdom.

The Return of the Prodigal Son (Luke 15,11–32).
Oil on canvas (1773).
Batoni, Pompeo (1708–1787)
Location: Kunsthistorisches Museum, Vienna, Austria

JESUS SAID THAT?

Modern expressions that find their source in the teachings of Christ.

Like a camel through the eye of a needle.

This is Jesus' famous description of how difficult it is for someone who has great wealth to recognize their need to trust God in order to enter the kingdom of heaven (Matthew 19:23–26).

Don't let the right hand know what the left hand is doing.

Jesus recommended that people should give in secret to the poor rather than advertise their charity (Matthew 6:3).

Do unto others as you would have them do unto you.

The "golden rule," as it is often called, was part of Jesus' teaching as recorded in Matthew (7:12) and Luke (6:31). Jesus' teachings in Matthew's Gospel (Chapters 5–7) and in Luke's Gospel (6:17–49) are often referred to as the "Sermon on the Mount" and the "Sermon on the Plain" respectively.

Be wise as serpents, harmless as doves.

This is the advice Jesus gave the twelve disciples before he sent them out on their own mission (Matthew 10:16).

Turn the other cheek . . .

This instruction urging us to shun vengeance is from the Sermon on the Mount (Matthew 5:39; Luke 6:29).

Judge not, lest you be judged.

This warning, included in the Sermon on the Mount, reminded Jesus' listeners that they would be judged by the same standard with which they judged others (Matthew 7:1).

An eye for an eye, a tooth for a tooth.

Jesus also quotes this ancient standard of Jewish justice (Exodus 21:24; Leviticus 24:20; Deuteronomy 19:21) in his Sermon on the Mount (Matthew 5:38, 39). His message of loving forgiveness introduces nonviolent resistance as a means for opposing evil.

Love your neighbor as yourself.

This remarkable call for compassion for others was included in the second part of Jesus' answer when asked to name the greatest commandment of all (Matthew 22:39; Mark 12:31). Jesus adapted this saying from Leviticus 19:18 in the Jewish Scriptures (known to Christians as the Old Testament).

The spirit is willing, but the flesh is weak.

Jesus said this to his disciples in the garden on the night before his death when they fell asleep instead of praying (Matthew 26:40, 41; Mark 14: 37, 38).

Oh ye of little faith!

Jesus said these words while he was walking on water in the midst of a storm! The disciple Peter, in a moment of great faith, had come out to meet Jesus—also walking on the water—but along the way he became afraid (Matthew 14:22–33).

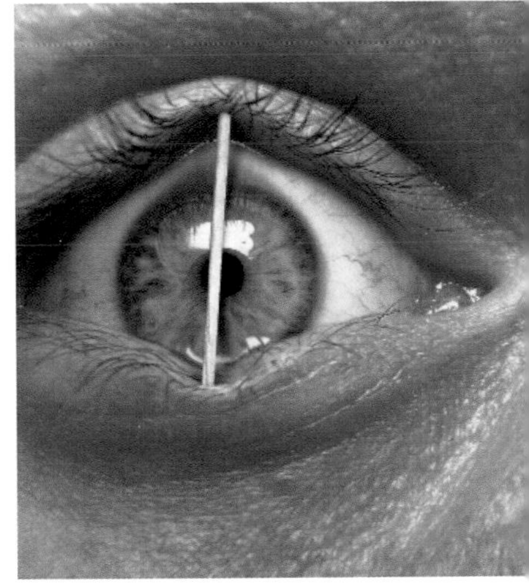

Get the plank out of your own eye before you talk about the speck in someone else's.

The Gospels according to Matthew and Luke record this saying as a part of Jesus' "Sermon on the Mount" or "Sermon on the Plain," specifically in his teaching on judgment (Matthew 7:3; Luke 6:41).

You can see the speck in your friend's eye, but you don't notice the log in your own eye.

Luke 6:41

Metaphors of the Kingdom

Jesus used metaphors and word pictures throughout his teaching to describe the ethics of those who are part of God's family. We may describe a decent, hardworking person as "the salt of the earth", (Matthew 5:13) but Jesus, who originated that term, had a much more specific meaning. He meant that his people should flavor and preserve the world with God's kingdom, just as salt was used in his day to flavor and preserve meat. Jesus used metaphors to describe his role in the kingdom, too, declaring himself the "bread of life" (John 6:35), who can satisfy the spiritual hunger of humanity in such a way that lives are transformed forever.

The Sermon on the Mount. Ca. 1680. Oil on canvas.
Chiari, Giuseppe (1654–1727)
Location: State Museum of Fine Art, Sebastopol, Ukraine

He Spoke With AUTHORITY

Jesus often assumed the role of a traveling preacher. He taught in cities as well as the countryside. As an observant Jew, he also taught in synagogues. Perhaps his most famous oration is the one called the Sermon on the Mount. As recorded in Matthew's Gospel, Jesus walked up a mountainside, presumably so he could be better seen and heard by a large crowd (Matthew 5:1). Luke, another Gospel writer, also records his version of these teachings, but he describes the site where Jesus was standing as a "level ground" (Luke 6:17).

The Gospel writers recorded Jesus' teachings in a variety of situations:

- When challenged by the religious establishment (John 8:12–18)
- When instructing his disciples (Luke 11:1–13)
- When faced with situations that required explanation or guidance (Matthew 10:5–15)
- When teaching in a formal setting (Luke 4:16–19)
- When saying a final farewell (John 13–16)
- When worshiping (Luke 22:14–20)

As God-in-the-flesh, Jesus repeatedly instructed his disciples on how to participate in God's kingdom. He not only expected them to follow "the golden rule" of treating others as they would want to be treated, but he also challenged his followers to radically rethink how they love those around them—especially those they didn't consider friends or who didn't treat them well (Matthew 5:43–48).

When someone hits you, Jesus urges you to "turn the other cheek" (Matthew 5:39). When someone asks you to give them something, he suggests that you give beyond what they ask or "go the extra mile" (Matthew 5:41). Jesus' mission was to change the status quo and usher in a whole new way of living and relating to God. When he said "store up your treasures in heaven" (Matthew 6:19–21) and "don't worry about tomorrow" (Matthew 6:25–34), he was challenging his disciples to trust that God would take care of their worldly needs if they sought the spiritual kingdom first.

When people ask you for something, give it to them.

Matthew 5:42

He Spoke in PRAYERS

Jesus often sought a place to pray away from the distractions of his work. He found strength and purpose in God's presence. There are deep theological mysteries that surround prayer—as humanity interacts with the divine— and Jesus' life reveals that making time to pray should be a priority to us.

Jesus prayed publicly as well. For instance, he gave thanks before breaking the bread and dividing the fish that would miraculously feed 5,000 people (Matthew 14:13–21; Mark 6:30–44; Luke 9:10-17; John 6:1–14). He also gave us instructions on the reasons we pray: we should not do so for show or simply out of habit (Matthew 6:5–7).

One of the most beautifully telling things Jesus said about prayer is that "your Father knows what you need even before you ask" (Matthew 6:8). In other words, nothing we could share with God could be news to him, because God knows what we need even better than we do. Nevertheless, sharing our needs with God is a vital part of that mysterious relationship.

In the Garden of Gethsemane, just before Jesus is arrested, he separates from the group of disciples to pray. In this riveting moment we see Jesus wrestle with his Father's will (Matthew 6:39; Mark 4:35, 36; Luke 22:41, 42). Then, coming back to his disciples, he finds they are sleeping instead of sharing the watch. "You want to do what is right, but you are weak," Jesus declares (Matthew 26:41; Mark 14:38). Understanding our own weakness and recognizing the importance of prayer, we should each strive to carve out time for one of life's primary spiritual disciplines and our best way of connecting with God.

When you pray, go into a room alone and close the door. Pray to your Father in private. He knows what is done in private and will reward you. When you pray, don't talk on and on as people do who don't know God. They think God likes to hear long prayers. Don't be like them. Your Father knows what you need even before you ask.

Matthew 6:6–8

Jesus praying.
Detail from *The Prayer in the Garden of Gethsemane*,
Byzantine fresco, 14th CE.
Location: Monastery Church, Ohrid, Macedonia

THE PRAYER OF *Unity*

JOHN 17:1, 15–26

After Jesus had finished speaking to his disciples, he looked up toward heaven and prayed: . . .

Father, I don't ask you to take my followers out of the world, but keep them safe from the evil one. They don't belong to this world, and neither do I. Your word is the truth. So let this truth make them completely yours. I am sending them into the world, just as you sent me. I have given myself completely for their sake, so that they may belong completely to the truth.

I am not praying just for these followers. I am also praying for everyone else who will have faith because of what my followers will say about me. I want all of them to be one with each other, just as I am one with you and you are one with me. I also want them to be one with us. Then the people of this world will believe that you sent me.

I have honored my followers in the same way that you honored me, in order that they may be one with each other, just as we are one. I am one with them, and you are one with me, so that they may become completely one. Then this world's people will know that you sent me. They will know that you love my followers as much as you love me.

Father, I want everyone you have given me to be with me, wherever I am. Then they will see the glory that you have given me, because you loved me before the world was created. Good Father, the people of this world don't know you. But I know you, and my followers know that you sent me. I told them what you are like, and I will tell them even more. Then the love that you have for me will become part of them, and I will be one with them.

THE LORD'S *Prayer*

Our Father in heaven, help us to honor your name. Come and set up your kingdom, so that everyone on earth will obey yo

Our Father

OUR FATHER IN HEAVEN,
HELP US TO HONOR
YOUR NAME.
COME AND SET UP
YOUR KINGDOM,
SO THAT EVERYONE ON EARTH
WILL OBEY YOU,
AS YOU ARE OBEYED
IN HEAVEN.
GIVE US OUR FOOD FOR TODAY.
FORGIVE US FOR DOING WRONG,
AS WE FORGIVE OTHERS.
KEEP US FROM BEING TEMPTED,
AND PROTECT US FROM EVIL.

(MATTHEW 6:9–13)

A QUOTE FROM THE BIBLE

MATTHEW 20:1–16

As Jesus was telling what the kingdom of heaven would be like, he said:

Early one morning a man went out to hire some workers for his vineyard. After he had agreed to pay them the usual amount for a day's work, he sent them off to his vineyard.

About nine that morning, the man saw some other people standing in the market with nothing to do. He promised to pay them what was fair, if they would work in his vineyard. So they went. At noon and again about three in the afternoon he returned to the market. And each time he made the same agreement with others who were loafing around with nothing to do.

Finally, about five in the afternoon the man went back and found some others standing there. He asked them, "Why have you been standing here all day long doing nothing?"

"Because no one has hired us," they answered. Then he told them to go work in his vineyard.

That evening the owner of the vineyard told the man in charge of the workers to call them in and give them their money. He also told the man to begin with the ones who were hired last. When the workers arrived, the ones who had been hired at five in the afternoon were given a full day's pay. The workers who had been hired first thought they would be given more than the others. But when they were given the same, they began complaining to the owner of the vineyard. They said, "The ones who were hired last worked for only one hour. But you paid them the same that you did us. And we worked in the hot sun all day long!"

The owner answered one of them, "Friend, I didn't cheat you. I paid you exactly what we agreed on. Take your money now and go! What business is it of yours if I want to pay them the same that I paid you? Don't I have the right to do what I want with my own money? Why should you be jealous, if I want to be generous?"

Jesus then said, "So it is. Everyone who is now last will be first, and everyone who is first will be last."

How many of Jesus' parables do you know?

Don't put your light under a bushel basket
Matthew 5:14–16; Mark 4:21–23; Luke 8:16–18

Putting a new patch on old clothes
Matthew 9:16; Mark 2:21; Luke 5:36

Putting new wine in old wineskins
Matthew 9:17; Mark 2:22; Luke 5:37–39

Faith as small as a mustard seed
Matthew 13:31–32; Mark 4:30–32; Luke 13:18–19

Parable of the . . .

Sower
Matthew 13:1–23; Mark 4:3–20; Luke 8:4–15

Weeds
Matthew 13:24–30, 36–43

Lost sheep
Matthew 18:10–14; Luke 15:3–7

Unmerciful official
Matthew 18:21–36

The obedient and disobedient sons
Matthew 21:28–32

Fig tree
Matthew 24:32–35; Mark 13:28–31; Luke 21:29–33

Good Samaritan
Luke 10:25–37

Faithful servant
Luke 12:42–48

Rich fool
Luke 12:13–21

Lost coin
Luke 15:8–10

Persistent widow
Luke 18:1–8

The Kingdom of Heaven is like . . .

A hidden treasure
Matthew 13:44

A pearl of great price
Matthew 13:45–46

A fisherman's net
Matthew 13:47–50

Yeast
Matthew 13:33; Luke 13:20–21

Workers in the vineyard
Matthew 20:1–16

A wedding banquet
Matthew 22:1–14

He Spoke in PARABLES

One of Jesus' favorite teaching strategies was to speak in parables, using simple stories to illustrate compelling truths. Some parables involved narratives, while others were simply short object lessons, much like proverbs.

Often the parables were prompted by the specific situation Jesus was facing at the time. He told the parable of the prodigal son (Luke 15:11–32) when some local Jewish religious leaders were assailing him for spending so much time in the company of reckless, irreligious people. He told the parable of the good Samaritan (Luke 10:25–37) when a lawyer asked for a definition of "neighbor." When Jesus was approached by a rich, young ruler who wanted to get to heaven, but couldn't bear to give up his wealth, Jesus drove home his point with a short parable about how difficult it is for a rich man to find salvation, saying this was as unlikely as seeing a camel pass through the eye of a needle (Matthew 19:23–26).

Jesus explained the kingdom of God over and over again in parables. It's like an expensive pearl, he said, or a fisherman's net, or a wedding banquet, among others. Sometimes Jesus taught in parables to enlighten; other times he did so to conceal. He told his disciples that those who had ears that were listening for spiritual truth would find that truth in the stories he told, while those who were only interested in Jesus' celebrity would simply hear a good story (Matthew 13:9–13).

The kingdom of heaven is like what happens when a shop owner is looking for fine pearls. After finding a very valuable one, the owner goes and sells everything in order to buy that pearl.

Matthew 13:45–46

He Spoke in Parables

The Scriptures say, 'Love the Lord your God with all your heart, soul, strength, and mind.' They also say, 'Love your neighbors as much as you love yourself.'

LUKE 10:25–37

THE GOOD SAMARITAN

AN EXPERT IN THE LAW OF MOSES STOOD UP AND ASKED JESUS A QUESTION TO SEE WHAT HE WOULD SAY. "TEACHER," HE ASKED, "WHAT MUST I DO TO HAVE ETERNAL LIFE?"

JESUS ANSWERED, "WHAT IS WRITTEN IN THE SCRIPTURES? HOW DO YOU UNDERSTAND THEM?"

THE MAN REPLIED, "THE SCRIPTURES SAY, 'LOVE THE LORD YOUR GOD WITH ALL YOUR HEART, SOUL, STRENGTH, AND MIND.' THEY ALSO SAY, 'LOVE YOUR NEIGHBORS AS MUCH AS YOU LOVE YOURSELF.' "

JESUS SAID, "YOU HAVE GIVEN THE RIGHT ANSWER. IF YOU DO THIS, YOU WILL HAVE ETERNAL LIFE."

BUT THE MAN WANTED TO SHOW THAT HE KNEW WHAT HE WAS TALKING ABOUT. SO HE ASKED JESUS, "WHO ARE MY NEIGHBORS?"

JESUS REPLIED:

AS A MAN WAS GOING DOWN FROM JERUSALEM TO JERICHO, ROBBERS ATTACKED HIM AND GRABBED EVERYTHING HE HAD. THEY BEAT HIM UP AND RAN OFF, LEAVING HIM HALF DEAD.

A PRIEST HAPPENED TO BE GOING DOWN THE SAME ROAD. BUT WHEN HE SAW THE MAN, HE WALKED BY ON THE OTHER SIDE. LATER A TEMPLE HELPER CAME TO THE SAME PLACE. BUT WHEN HE SAW THE MAN WHO HAD BEEN BEATEN UP, HE ALSO WENT BY ON THE OTHER SIDE.

A MAN FROM SAMARIA THEN CAME TRAVELING ALONG THAT ROAD. WHEN HE SAW THE MAN, HE FELT SORRY FOR HIM AND WENT OVER TO HIM. HE TREATED HIS WOUNDS WITH OLIVE OIL AND WINE AND BANDAGED THEM. THEN HE PUT HIM ON HIS OWN DONKEY AND TOOK HIM TO AN INN, WHERE HE TOOK CARE OF HIM. THE NEXT MORNING HE GAVE THE INNKEEPER TWO SILVER COINS AND SAID, "PLEASE TAKE CARE OF THE MAN. IF YOU SPEND MORE THAN THIS ON HIM, I WILL PAY YOU WHEN I RETURN."

THEN JESUS ASKED, "WHICH ONE OF THESE THREE PEOPLE WAS A REAL NEIGHBOR TO THE MAN WHO WAS BEATEN UP BY ROBBERS?"

THE EXPERT IN THE LAW OF MOSES ANSWERED, "THE ONE WHO SHOWED PITY."

JESUS SAID, "GO AND DO THE SAME!"

LUKE 15:11–24

THE PRODIGAL SON

JESUS TOLD THEM YET ANOTHER STORY:

ONCE A MAN HAD TWO SONS. THE YOUNGER SON SAID TO HIS FATHER, "GIVE ME MY SHARE OF THE PROPERTY." SO THE FATHER DIVIDED HIS PROPERTY BETWEEN HIS TWO SONS.

NOT LONG AFTER THAT, THE YOUNGER SON PACKED UP EVERYTHING HE OWNED AND LEFT FOR A FOREIGN COUNTRY, WHERE HE WASTED ALL HIS MONEY IN WILD LIVING. HE HAD SPENT EVERYTHING, WHEN A BAD FAMINE SPREAD THROUGH THAT WHOLE LAND. SOON HE HAD NOTHING TO EAT.

HE WENT TO WORK FOR A MAN IN THAT COUNTRY, AND THE MAN SENT HIM OUT TO TAKE CARE OF HIS PIGS. HE WOULD HAVE BEEN GLAD TO EAT WHAT THE PIGS WERE EATING, BUT NO ONE GAVE HIM A THING.

FINALLY, HE CAME TO HIS SENSES AND SAID, "MY FATHER'S WORKERS HAVE PLENTY TO EAT, AND HERE I AM, STARVING TO DEATH! I WILL GO TO MY FATHER AND SAY TO HIM, 'FATHER, I HAVE SINNED AGAINST GOD IN HEAVEN AND AGAINST YOU. I AM NO LONGER GOOD ENOUGH TO BE CALLED YOUR SON. TREAT ME LIKE ONE OF YOUR WORKERS.' "

THE YOUNGER SON GOT UP AND STARTED BACK TO HIS FATHER. BUT WHEN HE WAS STILL A LONG WAY OFF, HIS FATHER SAW HIM AND FELT SORRY FOR HIM. HE RAN TO HIS SON AND HUGGED AND KISSED HIM.

THE SON SAID, "FATHER, I HAVE SINNED AGAINST GOD IN HEAVEN AND AGAINST YOU. I AM NO LONGER GOOD ENOUGH TO BE CALLED YOUR SON."

BUT HIS FATHER SAID TO THE SERVANTS, "HURRY AND BRING THE BEST CLOTHES AND PUT THEM ON HIM. GIVE HIM A RING FOR HIS FINGER AND SANDALS FOR HIS FEET. GET THE BEST CALF AND PREPARE IT, SO WE CAN EAT AND CELEBRATE. THIS SON OF MINE WAS DEAD, BUT HAS NOW COME BACK TO LIFE. HE WAS LOST AND HAS NOW BEEN FOUND." AND THEY BEGAN TO CELEBRATE.

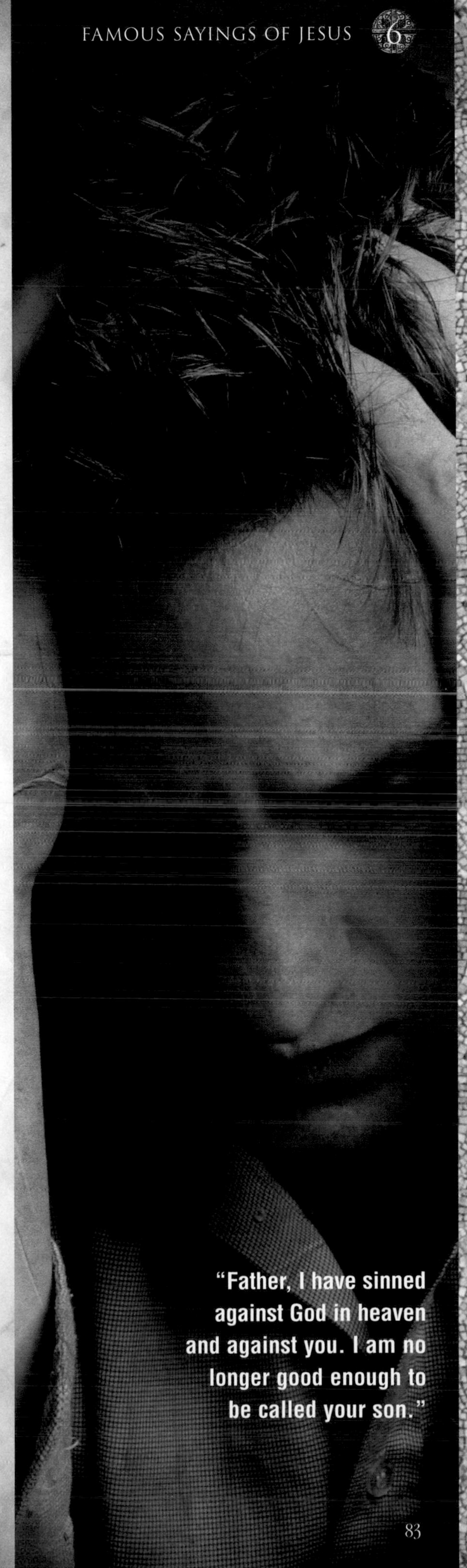

"Father, I have sinned against God in heaven and against you. I am no longer good enough to be called your son."

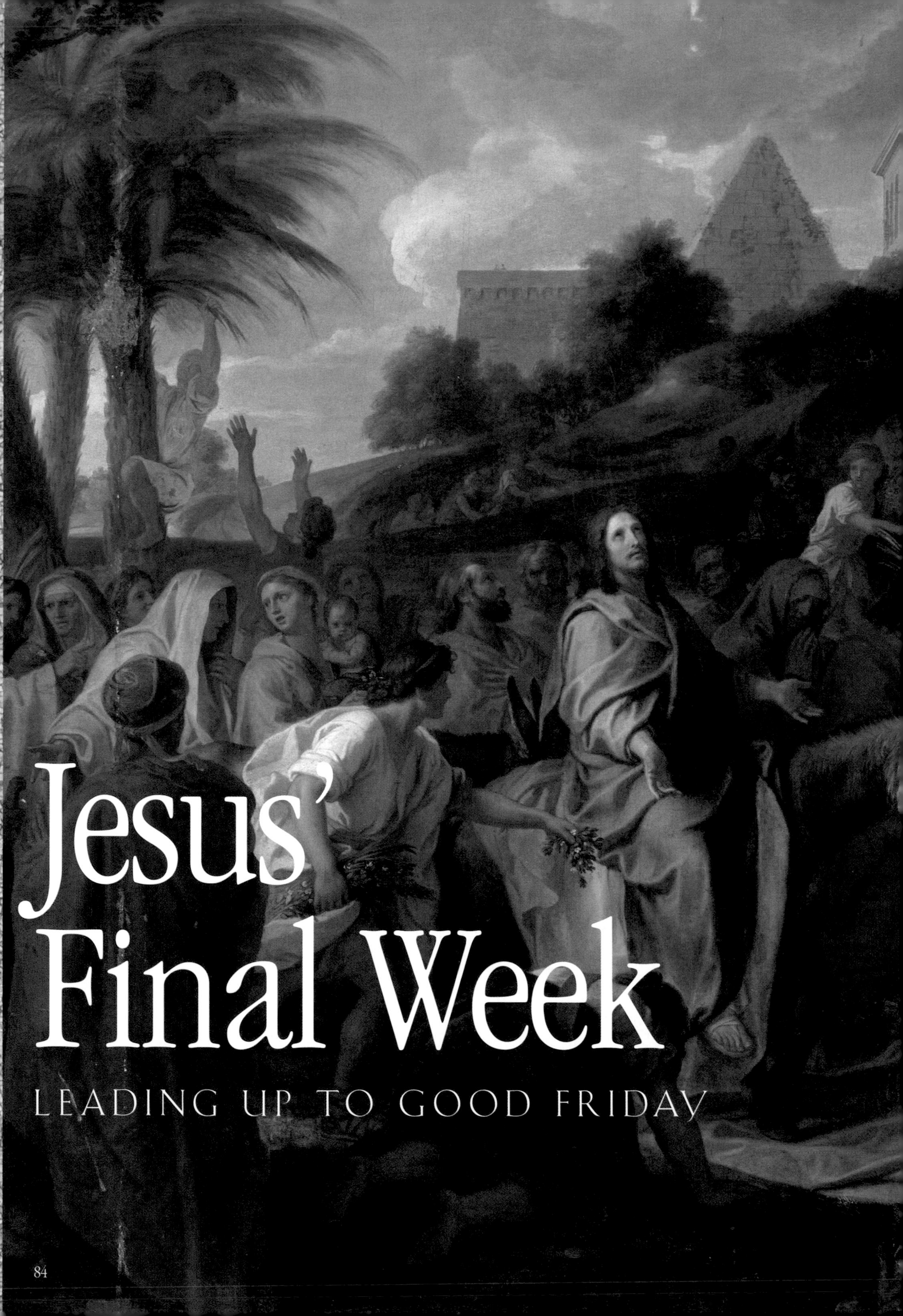

Jesus' Final Week

LEADING UP TO GOOD FRIDAY

The last few days of Jesus' life before his crucifixion and resurrection were filled with drama and controversy—and with historic events we still commemorate today. Last words were spoken. Blood and tears were shed. Jesus' mission was accomplished. The events of that week have been retold, studied, and pondered time and again through the centuries. They trace a circular trajectory, moving from the jubilation of Palm Sunday to the horror of Good Friday to the astonishment of Easter Sunday.

The seven days before Easter Sunday, the day Christians celebrate Jesus' resurrection from the grave, are known today as Holy Week, or Passion Week. The Eastern Orthodox Church calls this span the Great Week. Most of our contemporary traditions related to Holy Week are observed in parallel to this last week of Jesus' life.

Holy Week begins with Palm Sunday, or Passion Sunday—the day of Jesus' glorious entrance into Jerusalem. Today palm fronds are often handed out during Palm Sunday services, recalling the cheering townspeople who threw palm fronds, leaves, and their own cloaks in front of the miracle-working preacher as he rode into the city on a donkey. At that time, such a ceremonial entrance was the customary welcome for any renowned hero or ruler entering a large city.

Monday through Wednesday of Holy Week note several specific events of Jesus' life. Holy Monday marks his "cleansing of the Temple," when he threw out the dishonest money-changers who were profaning the sacred place. Holy Tuesday recalls how he traveled with his disciples to the Mount of Olives, where he taught them about the Last Days. On Holy Wednesday (in some places called Spy Wednesday) his turncoat disciple, Judas Iscariot, first conspired to betray Jesus for thirty pieces of silver (Luke 22:1–5).

What we now refer to as Maundy Thursday, or Holy Thursday, commemorates Jesus' Last Supper with his disciples, which inaugurated the contemporary practices of the Eucharist or Holy Communion. The word Maundy is derived from the Latin *novum mandatum* ("new command") based on Jesus' words recorded in John 13:34. Maundy Thursday services often include a ceremony of the washing of feet, in memory of Jesus' washing his disciples' feet, a task normally performed by servants in those times. Another custom in many contemporary Maundy Thursday services involves stripping the church altar of all linen and light.

Good Friday recalls Jesus' crucifixion and burial. Some churches have "Tenebrae" services, or services of darkness, to commemorate Jesus' suffering and death on the cross. During somber Holy Saturday, Christians remember the period of time when Jesus rested in the grave, and the day culminates in evening services, known as the Great or Easter Vigil, anticipating Easter Sunday.

Christ's Entry into Jerusalem.
Oil on canvas.
Le Brun, Charles (1619–1690)
Location: Musee d'Art et d'Industrie, Saint-Etienne, France

Palm Sunday

THE TRIUMPHAL ENTRANCE

Today, Palm Sunday is observed as the sixth and last Sunday in Lent and the first day of Holy Week. Always occurring seven days before Easter, the day commemorates Jesus Christ's triumphal entrance into Jerusalem in the last week of his life. (See Matthew 21:1–11; Mark 11:1–11; Luke 19:28–44; John 12:12–19.)

Everyone in Jerusalem, celebrate and shout! Your king has won a victory, and he is coming to you. He is humble and rides on a donkey; he comes on the colt of a donkey.

Zechariah 9:9

The Entry of Christ into Jerusalem.
Mosaic.
The Master of the Cappella Palatina (1150)
Location: Palermo, Italy

The Christian church believes that the events of Palm Sunday fulfill the prophecy found in Zechariah 9:9. Jesus was the gentle Savior, riding a humble donkey into Jerusalem to announce peace and salvation.

In Jewish tradition, the palm branch was a symbol of triumph and of victory, and is treated in other parts of the Bible as such (e.g. Leviticus 23:40 and Revelation 7:9). Because of this, the scene of the crowd greeting Jesus by waving palms and carpeting his path with them has given Palm Sunday its name.

On that day, crowds of Jesus' admirers cried "Hosanna" ("Save us!") and hailed Jesus as heir to King David and thus the Messiah that God had promised. They covered his path with cloaks and palm fronds, symbols of victory and honor. Yet within days, some of these same people would be among those jeering Christ and calling for his crucifixion.

Palm Sunday summons us to behold our king: the Word of God made flesh. We are called to behold him not simply as the one who came to us once riding on a donkey, but as the one who is always present, revealing himself to us in every act of love, kindness and mercy. He comes not only to deliver us from death by his sacrifice on the cross and resurrection, but also to have fellowship with him. He is the king, who liberates us from the darkness of sin and the bondage of death. Palm Sunday summons us to behold our king: the vanquisher of death and the giver of life.

A QUOTE FROM THE BIBLE

MARK 11:1–11

Jesus and his disciples reached Bethpage and Bethany near the Mount of Olives. When they were getting close to Jerusalem, Jesus sent two of them on ahead. He told them, "Go into the next village. As soon as you enter it, you will find a young donkey that has never been ridden. Untie the donkey and bring it here. If anyone asks why you are doing this, say, 'The Lord needs it and will soon bring it back.' "

The disciples left and found the donkey tied near a door that faced the street. While they were untying it, some of the people standing there asked, "Why are you untying the donkey?" They told them what Jesus had said, and the people let them take it.

The disciples led the donkey to Jesus. They put some of their clothes on its back, and Jesus got on. Many people spread clothes on the road, while others spread branches they had cut from the fields.

In front of Jesus and behind him, people went along shouting,

"Hooray!
God bless the one who comes
in the name of the Lord!
God bless the coming kingdom
of our ancestor David.
Hooray for God
in heaven above!"

After Jesus had gone to Jerusalem, he went into the temple and looked around at everything. But since it was already late in the day, he went back to Bethany with the twelve disciples.

Preparing a Feast

JESUS' LAST PASSOVER CELEBRATION

Jesus' final week was set in front of the backdrop of the preparations for the Passover Feast, a yearly festival that prompted many first-century Jews to travel to Jerusalem. The feast, which commemorated God's dramatic provision in the history of the Jewish nation, involved the sacrifice of an innocent lamb.

The origin of the Passover feast is found in ancient Egypt, where the family of Jacob (also called Israel) sought refuge from a famine. There, over hundreds of years, that family grew into a nation of Israelite people enslaved by the Egyptians (Exodus 1:6–14). The Old Testament book of Exodus tells us that when Moses asked for the freedom of these enslaved people, God sent a series of plagues to convince Egypt's king to comply.

In the last of these plagues, death swept across Egypt, taking the firstborn of every family and herd. The only firstborns spared were those belonging to Israelite families who sacrificed an innocent lamb and marked their doorposts with the blood of that lamb.

God instructed the people to commemorate the Passover year from then on. Each time a Jewish family celebrates the Passover, they recount the story and relive the event with a memorial meal.

TELL THE PEOPLE OF ISRAEL

THAT ON THE TENTH DAY OF THIS MONTH THE HEAD OF EACH FAMILY MUST CHOOSE A LAMB OR A YOUNG GOAT FOR HIS FAMILY TO EAT. IF ANY FAMILY IS TOO SMALL TO EAT THE WHOLE ANIMAL, THEY MUST SHARE IT WITH THEIR NEXT-DOOR NEIGHBORS. CHOOSE EITHER A SHEEP OR A GOAT, BUT IT MUST BE A ONE-YEAR-OLD MALE THAT HAS NOTHING WRONG WITH IT. AND IT MUST BE LARGE ENOUGH FOR EVERYONE TO HAVE SOME OF THE MEAT.

EACH FAMILY MUST TAKE CARE OF ITS ANIMAL UNTIL THE EVENING OF THE FOURTEENTH DAY OF THE MONTH, WHEN THE ANIMALS ARE TO BE KILLED. SOME OF THE BLOOD MUST BE PUT ON THE TWO DOORPOSTS AND ABOVE THE DOOR OF EACH HOUSE WHERE THE ANIMALS ARE TO BE EATEN. THAT NIGHT THE ANIMALS ARE TO BE ROASTED AND EATEN, TOGETHER WITH BITTER HERBS AND THIN BREAD MADE WITHOUT

YEAST. DON'T EAT THE MEAT RAW OR BOILED. THE ENTIRE ANIMAL, INCLUDING ITS HEAD, LEGS, AND INSIDES, MUST BE ROASTED. EAT WHAT YOU WANT THAT NIGHT, AND THE NEXT MORNING BURN WHATEVER IS LEFT. WHEN YOU EAT THE MEAL, BE DRESSED AND READY TO TRAVEL. HAVE YOUR SANDALS ON, CARRY YOUR WALKING STICK IN YOUR HAND, AND EAT QUICKLY. THIS IS THE PASSOVER FESTIVAL IN HONOR OF ME, YOUR LORD.

THAT SAME NIGHT I WILL PASS THROUGH EGYPT AND KILL THE FIRST-BORN SON IN EVERY FAMILY AND THE FIRST-BORN MALE OF ALL ANIMALS. I AM THE LORD, AND I WILL PUNISH THE GODS OF EGYPT. THE BLOOD ON THE HOUSES WILL SHOW ME WHERE YOU LIVE, AND WHEN I SEE THE BLOOD, I WILL PASS OVER YOU. THEN YOU WON'T BE BOTHERED BY THE TERRIBLE DISASTERS I WILL BRING ON EGYPT.

REMEMBER THIS DAY AND CELEBRATE IT EACH YEAR AS A FESTIVAL IN MY HONOR. EXODUS 12:3-14

Carving of the Last Supper on Barcelona's Sagrada Familia

A QUOTE FROM THE BIBLE

MARK 14:22–26

During the meal Jesus took some bread in his hands. He blessed the bread and broke it. Then he gave it to his disciples and said, "Take this. It is my body."

Jesus picked up a cup of wine and gave thanks to God. He gave it to his disciples, and they all drank some. Then he said, "This is my blood, which is poured out for many people, and with it God makes his agreement. From now on I will not drink any wine, until I drink new wine in God's kingdom." Then they sang a hymn and went out to the Mount of Olives.

Maundy Thursday

LOVE ONE ANOTHER

While churches have traditionally used the Easter Vigil as a time to welcome new members through transfer or baptism, some churches see an obvious connection between the footwashing ceremony and baptism. For them the Holy Thursday service is a time to observe the baptism of new believers and the reconciliation of those returning to the faith.

Maundy Thursday's name comes from an anthem sung in Latin in some liturgies on that day: *Mandatum novum do vobis* ("I am giving you a new command," from John 13:34). This new commandment was Christ's radical call for each of us to love one another as Jesus loved: unconditionally and sacrificially.

On this solemn day, Christians recall Jesus' Last Supper with his disciples, in which he inaugurated the Eucharist, or Holy Communion. On this evening before the Jewish weekly Sabbath was to begin, he and his disciples gathered in an upper room to observe the Passover meal. Jesus offered the disciples bread, calling it his body. He then offered them wine, calling it his blood. He asked them to eat the bread and drink the wine together to remember him. Thus, in various styles and forms, many churches today still remember Jesus in this way, sharing his body and blood. Those who take part believe they are entering into communion not only with their fellow worshipers today, but with their predecessors centuries ago, Christ and his disciples.

According to John's Gospel (13:8), Jesus washed the feet of his disciples, telling them, "If I don't wash you, you don't really belong to me." This provided a powerful lesson for these men who had walked closely with him.

Humbling himself before them, their leader took on the role of a servant, showing them—by his example, rather than simply telling them—that the requirements of those who seek the kingdom of God can be surprising and that humility is a virtue. Jesus' actions have motivated many churches to include a foot-washing service on Holy Thursday, to emphasize Christ's message of personal humility and service to others.

There was treachery, too, at this last meal: the disciple Judas Iscariot departed the company to tell the authorities of Jesus' plans (John 13:21–30). Later, Jesus agonized in the Garden of Gethsemane as he prayed, knowing he had been betrayed by Judas (Luke 22:39–48).

The service often involves stripping the altar of all light and decoration, in preparation for the solemn severity of the events of Good Friday.

8

THE PASSION

Jesus' Final Week

THE PATH TO CRUCIFIXION

Christians commemorate Jesus' final days on earth by observing the solemnity of Good Friday and anticipating the joy of Jesus' resurrection that is celebrated on Easter Sunday. Often referred to as The Passion, the last days and death of Jesus have been reenacted repeatedly through the years in various forms and manners, from movie screens to rural church auditoriums, from street processions to vast outdoor pageants.

The account of Jesus' trials and crucifixion make up much of the closing chapters of the four Gospels, the first four books of the New Testament. While those recorded details have remained the same since they were first written, we have come to understand more and more about them as scholars have helped advance our understanding of cultural history and as we learn to carefully read ancient texts. Thus, it is important to continue to revisit the biblical accounts of the story and to explore the significance of those accounts to our lives today.

Christ Presented to the People (Ecce Homo).
Oil on canvas.
Sodoma, Giovanni Antonio Bazzi, called Il (1477–1549)
The Metropolitan Museum of Art, New York, NY, U.S.A.

THE TIMELINE

THE EVENTS LEADING UP TO EASTER

1 Sunday*

Jesus' triumphal entry into Jerusalem

The next day a large crowd was in Jerusalem for Passover. When they heard that Jesus was coming for the festival, they took palm branches and went out to greet him. They shouted,

"Hooray! God bless the one who comes in the name of the Lord! God bless the King of Israel!"

(John 12:12-13)

2 Monday

Jesus runs the merchants out of the temple

When Jesus entered the temple, he started chasing out the people who were selling things. He told them, "The Scriptures say, 'My house should be a place of worship.' But you have made it a place where robbers hide!" Each day, Jesus kept on teaching in the temple. So the chief priests, the teachers of the Law of Moses, and some other important people tried to have him killed. But they could not find a way to do it, because everyone else was eager to listen to him.

(Luke 19:45-48)

3 Tuesday

The conflicts in the temple

The Pharisees got together with Herod's followers. Then they sent some men to trick Jesus into saying something wrong. They went to him and said, "Teacher, we know that you are honest. You treat everyone with the same respect, no matter who they are. And you teach the truth about what God wants people to do. Tell us, should we pay taxes to the Emperor or not?" Jesus knew what they were up to, and he said, "Why are you trying to test me? Show me a coin!" They brought him a silver coin, and he asked, "Whose picture and name are on it?" "The Emperor's," they answered. Then Jesus told them, "Give the Emperor what belongs to him and give God what belongs to God." The men were amazed at Jesus.

(Mark 12:13-17)

4 Wednesday

The Plot for Jesus' death grows

It was now two days before Passover and the Festival of Thin Bread. The chief priests and the teachers of the Law of Moses were planning how they could sneak around and have Jesus arrested and put to death. They were saying, "We must not do it during the festival, because the people will riot."

(Mark 14:1-2)

**While we do not know the actual days on which each event occurred, here is a traditional listing of events from the passion week.*

5 Thursday

Last Supper

Betrayal and arrest

Trial before Annas

Trial before Caiphas

During the meal Jesus took some bread in his hands. He blessed the bread and broke it. Then he gave it to his disciples and said, "Take this and eat it. This is my body." Jesus picked up a cup of wine and gave thanks to God. He then gave it to his disciples and said, "Take this and drink it. This is my blood, and with it God makes his agreement with you. It will be poured out, so that many people will have their sins forgiven.

(Matthew 26:26-28)

6 Friday

Morning trial before the Sanhedrin

Trial before Pilate

Trial before Herod

Final trial before Pilate

Crucifixion and burial

Jesus knew that he had now finished his work. And in order to make the Scriptures come true, he said, "I am thirsty!" A jar of cheap wine was there. Someone then soaked a sponge with the wine and held it up to Jesus' mouth on the stem of a hyssop plant. After Jesus drank the wine, he said, "Everything is done!" He bowed his head and died.

(John 19:28-30)

7 Saturday

Jesus lies in the tomb

On the next day, which was a Sabbath, the chief priests and the Pharisees went together to Pilate. They said, "Sir, we remember what this liar said while he was still alive. He claimed in three days he would come back from death. So please order the tomb to be carefully guarded for three days. If you don't, his disciples may come and steal his body. They will tell the people he has been raised to life, and this last lie will be worse than the first one." Pilate said to them, "All right, take some of your soldiers and guard the tomb as well as you know how." So they sealed it tight and placed soldiers there to guard it.

(Matthew 27:62-66)

8 Sunday

Resurrection

The Sabbath was over, and it was almost daybreak on Sunday when Mary Magdalene and the other Mary went to see the tomb. Suddenly a strong earthquake struck, and the Lord's angel came down from heaven. He rolled away the stone and sat on it. The angel looked as bright as lightning, and his clothes were white as snow. The guards shook from fear and fell down, as though they were dead. The angel said to the women, "Don't be afraid! I know you are looking for Jesus, who was nailed to a cross. He isn't here! God has raised him to life, just as Jesus said he would. Come, see the place where his body was lying."

(Matthew 28:1-6)

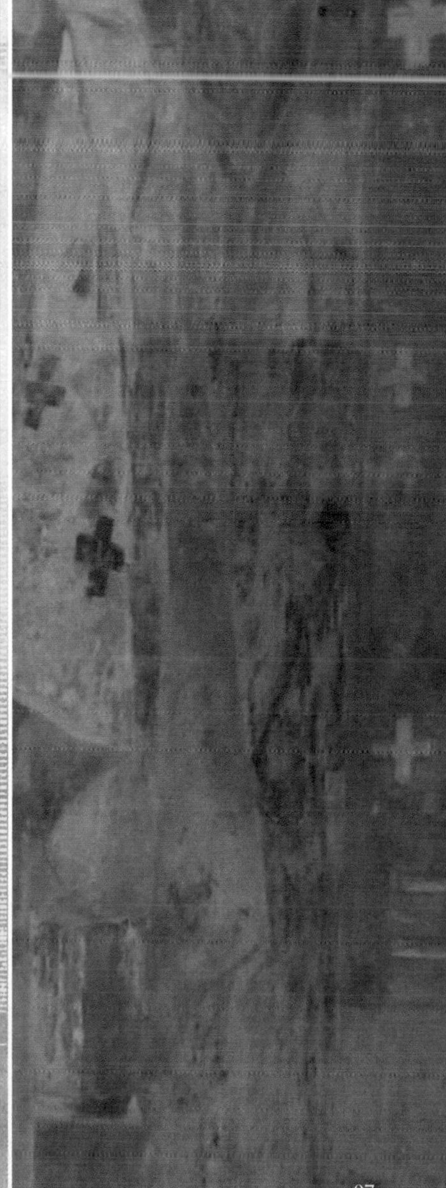

THE TRIALS

The trials of Jesus are described toward the end of all four Gospel accounts, though the sequence of events is different in John's Gospel when compared to Matthew's, Mark's, and Luke's. The trials took place in a haphazard, almost ping-pong fashion, as the case was switched, in midstream, between courts and judges.

This was not unusual in Judea at the time, where the justice system was controlled by representatives of the mighty Roman Empire. It worked to the advantage of imperial Rome to let the Jews settle as many smaller disputes as possible on their own. Less serious cases were tried in a Jewish court that had limited powers, particularly in terms of capital punishment. More significant cases were tried in the Roman court. It was between these two courts that Jesus' fate seemed to hang in the balance.

First Trial: The Religious Leaders

The temple guards, chief priests, and Jewish elders came at nightfall to the Mount of Olives on Jerusalem's outskirts to arrest Jesus. Judas Iscariot, one of Jesus' inner circle of twelve disciples, had betrayed him for money. Jesus' closest followers, intimidated and afraid, fled the scene and watched fearfully from a distance.

In the courtyard of Caiaphas, the High Priest, the council debated ways to silence Jesus, whose claims to be the Son of God undermined their authority at every turn. Outside, the guards decided to have a little fun with their captive. They blindfolded and taunted the miracle-worker, demanding he mystically identify each man who hit him. Jesus, turning the other cheek, remained silent. Finally, at dawn, Caiaphas asked: "Are you the Messiah, the Son of God?" (Matthew 26:63). When Jesus refused to deny that he was the long-promised savior of the Jews, the leaders had what they needed: a charge of blasphemy, claiming equality with God.

Second Trial: Pilate

The mob, sensing blood, carried Jesus along to the Roman governor, Pontius Pilate. Rome had ruled Jerusalem and the surrounding Mediterranean for the past 80 years, and the religious leaders needed the Empire's political approval if Jesus were to be handed the death penalty.

Yet Pilate had difficulty finding fault with Jesus; he believed the Jewish authorities were jealous, threatened by this itinerant preacher's growing reputation as a great spiritual leader.

Third Trial: Herod

Luke's Gospel alone reports on a third trial before Herod (Luke 23:6–12). Upon hearing that Jesus was a Galilean and thus technically outside his jurisdiction, Pilate was happy to outsource the case; he handed it over to Herod, the northern governor who had come to Jerusalem for the spring festivals. (Herod is a family name. This is a different Herod, though a descendant, from the king of Judea who sought to kill the child Jesus shortly after his birth.)

Delighted to finally see the famous wonder-worker, Herod barraged Jesus with questions and hoped he would perform a miracle. Again, Jesus remained silent. His dogged refusal to submit to Herod's will enraged the official, and he switched from cajoling his captive to venomously mocking him. Burning with hatred, the priests, Herod, his soldiers, and the angry mob threw an elegant robe over Jesus and returned him to Pilate in disgust.

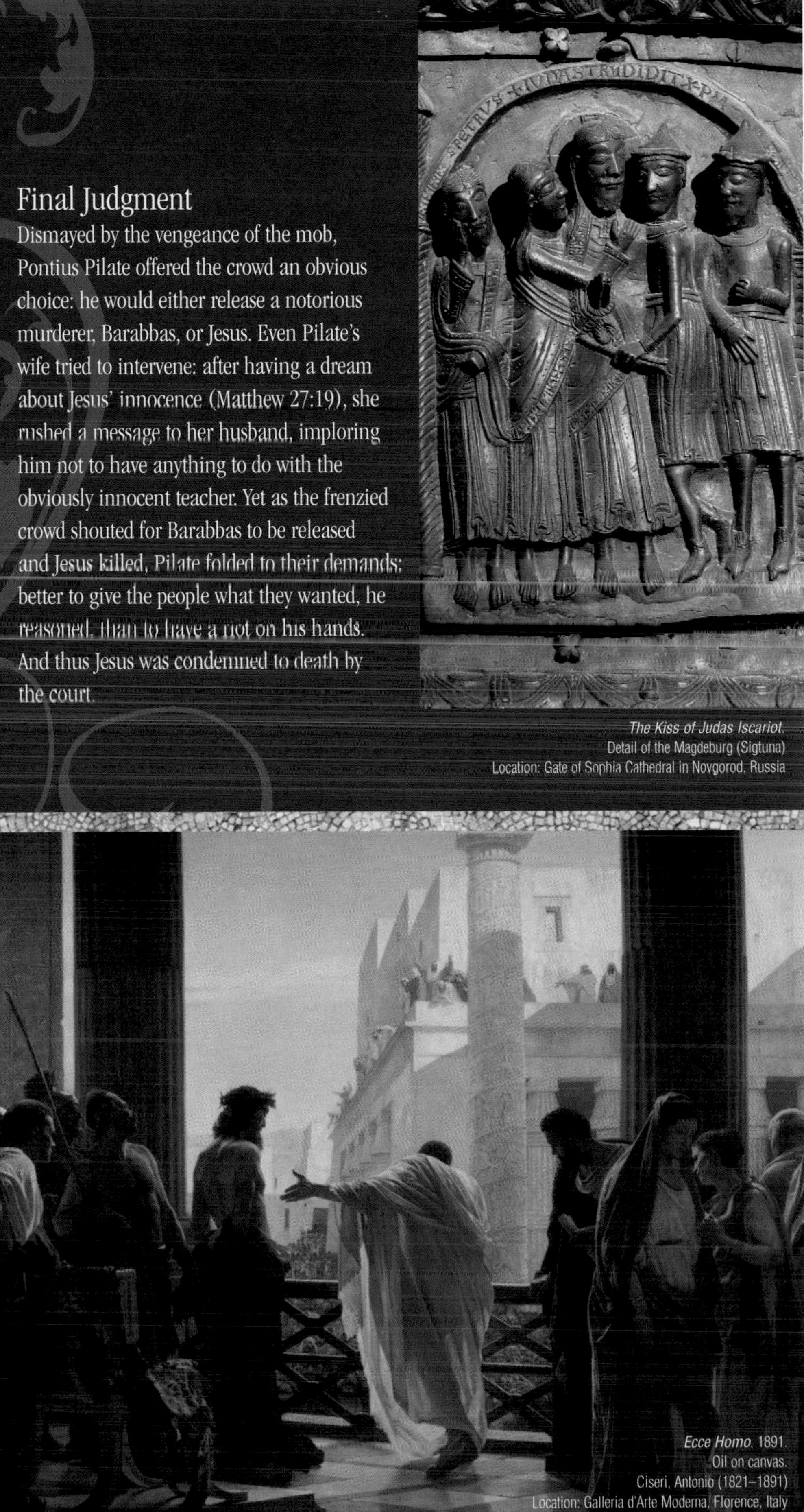

Final Judgment

Dismayed by the vengeance of the mob, Pontius Pilate offered the crowd an obvious choice: he would either release a notorious murderer, Barabbas, or Jesus. Even Pilate's wife tried to intervene: after having a dream about Jesus' innocence (Matthew 27:19), she rushed a message to her husband, imploring him not to have anything to do with the obviously innocent teacher. Yet as the frenzied crowd shouted for Barabbas to be released and Jesus killed, Pilate folded to their demands; better to give the people what they wanted, he reasoned, than to have a riot on his hands. And thus Jesus was condemned to death by the court.

The Kiss of Judas Iscariot.
Detail of the Magdeburg (Sigtuna)
Location: Gate of Sophia Cathedral in Novgorod, Russia

Ecce Homo. 1891.
Oil on canvas.
Ciseri, Antonio (1821–1891)
Location: Galleria d'Arte Moderna, Florence, Italy

Why the Accusations?

In order to bring a case against Jesus before Pilate and Herod, the religious leaders had to accuse him of a serious crime. They understood that their primary accusation—that Jesus had blasphemed when he claimed to be God—would matter little to the secular Romans. Therefore, the religious elders turned the charge into a claim that Jesus wanted to be king and had incited his followers to rebellion. These grave allegations would certainly command Pilate's attention, for the charges painted Jesus as a rebel against Rome, and Pilate's primary duty was to maintain imperial rule and keep order among Rome's subjects, the Judeans.

Under Roman law, Caesar alone must be worshiped as both king and deity. Because of this, the additional accusation that Jesus opposed paying taxes to Caesar (an inaccurate twisting of his words) was an offense that demanded punishment. Yet, as is obvious from Pilate's puzzlement at the accusations, it was by no means certain that this charge, even if found to be true, was so serious as to demand Jesus' execution.

Of course, the real issue throughout Jesus' ministry was that he challenged the religious establishment's traditional practices, as well as their claims of righteousness. While it was the leaders' role to debunk false messiahs, their opposition to Jesus, as it is described in the four Gospels, seemed to focus on what they saw as his highly unconventional message that everyone could participate in the kingdom of God, a message that effectively bypassed the elders' authority.

A QUOTE FROM THE BIBLE

MARK 15:22–37

The soldiers took Jesus to Golgotha, which means "Place of a Skull." There they gave him some wine mixed with a drug to ease the pain, but he refused to drink it.

They nailed Jesus to a cross and gambled to see who would get his clothes. It was about nine o'clock in the morning when they nailed him to the cross. On it was a sign that told why he was nailed there. It read, "This is the King of the Jews." The soldiers also nailed two criminals on crosses, one to the right of Jesus and the other to his left.

People who passed by said terrible things about Jesus. . . .

The chief priests and the teachers of the Law of Moses also made fun of Jesus. . . .

The two criminals also said cruel things to Jesus. . . .

About noon the sky turned dark and stayed that way until around three o'clock. Then about that time Jesus shouted, "Eloi, Eloi, lema sabachthani?" which means, "My God, my God, why have you deserted me?"

Some of the people standing there heard Jesus and said, "He is calling for Elijah." One of them ran and grabbed a sponge. After he had soaked it in wine, he put it on a stick and held it up to Jesus. He said, "Let's wait and see if Elijah will come and take him down!" Jesus shouted and then died.

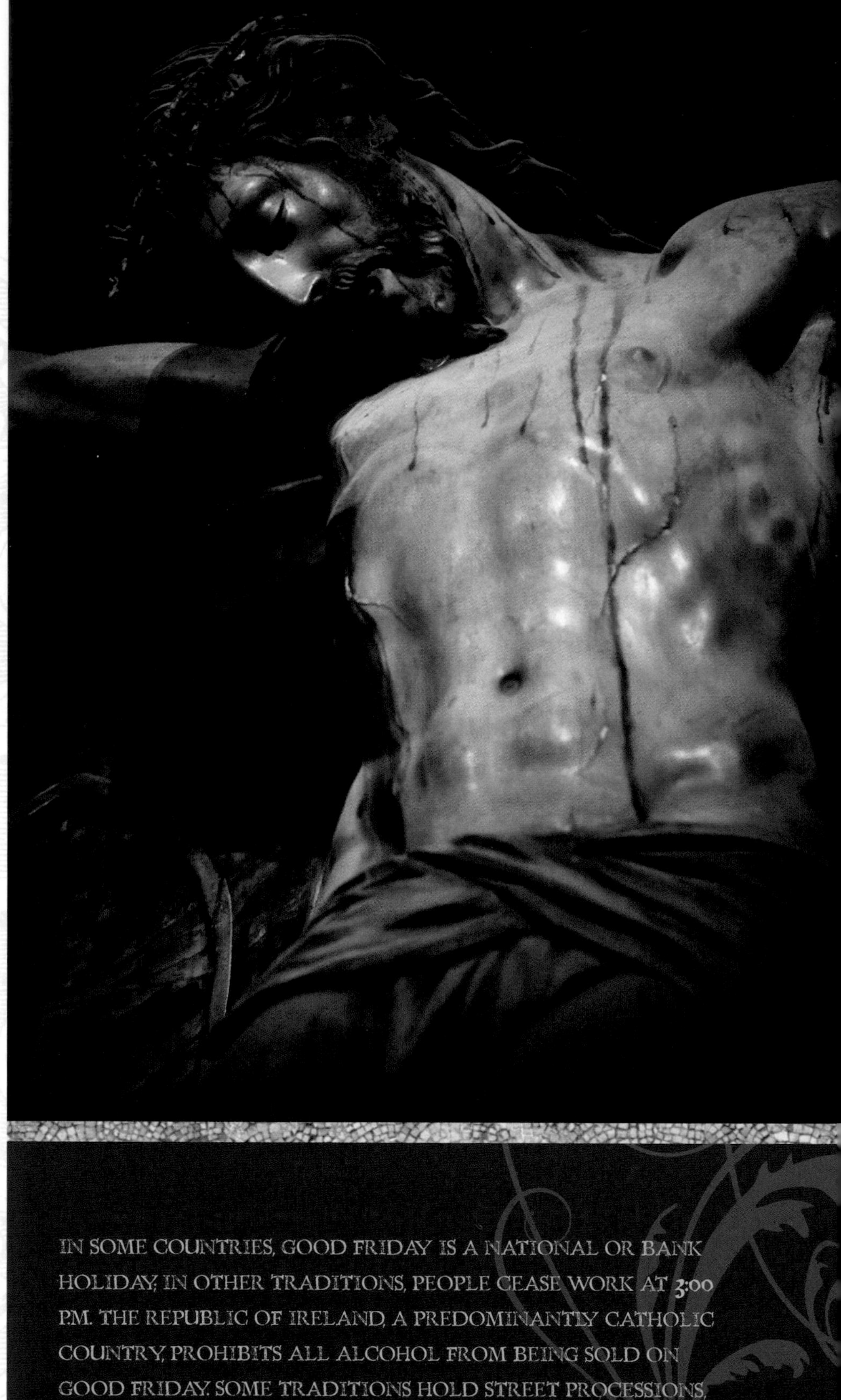

IN SOME COUNTRIES, GOOD FRIDAY IS A NATIONAL OR BANK HOLIDAY; IN OTHER TRADITIONS, PEOPLE CEASE WORK AT 3:00 P.M. THE REPUBLIC OF IRELAND, A PREDOMINANTLY CATHOLIC COUNTRY, PROHIBITS ALL ALCOHOL FROM BEING SOLD ON GOOD FRIDAY. SOME TRADITIONS HOLD STREET PROCESSIONS, RECALLING JESUS' JOURNEY TO HIS DEATH.

EASTERN ORTHODOX CHRISTIANS CUSTOMARILY DO NOT EAT ON THIS DAY OR ON HOLY SATURDAY. THE ROMAN CATHOLIC CHURCH OBSERVES SOME FASTING AS WELL.

Good Friday is the Friday before Easter. This day commemorates the crucifixion and death of Jesus on a hill outside Jerusalem known as Golgotha, which means "Place of the Skull."

Since Jewish custom measures a day as running from sunset to sunset, Good Friday for Jesus and his disciples began after sundown of Maundy Thursday. Following the Last Supper, Jesus was arrested in the Garden of Gethsemane, where he was praying alone. He was dragged before the ruling religious council, known as the Sanhedrin, who convicted him of blasphemy (falsely claiming to be God). But this body did not have the authority to hand down a sentence of capital punishment, so during the early hours of Friday, the Sanhedrin sent Jesus to the Roman governor of Judea, Pontius Pilate.

Pilate, in turn, ordered Jesus to appear before Herod, the Roman-appointed Jewish ruler of Galilee, Jesus' home area. Herod quickly sent Jesus back, disappointed when the man who called himself the Son of God refused to perform any miracles. Frustrated, Pilate finally consented to the Sanhedrin's wishes and the demands of the crowd, and agreed to order the death sentence for Jesus.

Jesus was crucified and hung on the cross from the sixth hour to the ninth hour, or from noon to 3 p.m. John's Gospel notes that this coincided with the time the Passover lambs were being prepared for the sacrifice. His death was agonizing and painful; it is described in the Bible as both a terror and a triumph (Matthew 27:45–56; Mark 15:22–41; Luke 23:44–49; John 19:28–30).

After Jesus drank the wine, he said, "Everything is done!" He bowed his head and died. John 19:30

Good Friday Procession in Sicily

Calvario in Sicily

THE CRUCIFIXION

In the last 2,000 years, artists from many traditions and cultures around the world have created representations of Christ's suffering on the cross—in paintings, in sculptures, in drawings. Yet even the most macabre of such images often tell us more about the era in which they were created than they do about the actual physical ordeal that Jesus endured.

In fact, after the trials had concluded, with the crucifixion still ahead, Jesus' back was already flayed open from the whipping some writers refer to as the Roman Half-Death. This term was more fact than metaphor: half of the men who suffered this extreme round of scourging died. As Jesus was taken to be crucified, blood loss had already weakened him to the point that the soldiers had to drag a man from the crowd, Simon from Cyrene, to help carry the cross.

Romans usually tied criminals to the cross, knowing that the victim's weakness from beatings and blood loss would make it increasingly difficult to lift his body enough to take even a shallow breath. Thus crucifixion was actually a form of hanging—it cut off the victim's air flow as he lost his strength. Sometimes a guard would have mercy and break the sufferer's legs to end the torturous pain of the slow death.

Nailed to the cross rather than tied to it, Jesus would receive no respite from the misery of his death. His mother stood nearby weeping, and some of his closest friends looked on in silence, keenly aware that none of them had spoken up in his defense. The soldiers—who were just carrying out another day's routine executions—sat gambling, dividing up the personal effects of the dying men who were beyond all comfort or need of material things.

In addition to suffering extreme physical distress, Jesus also endured the shame of dying alone and seemingly powerless, high on a hill, exposed for all to see.

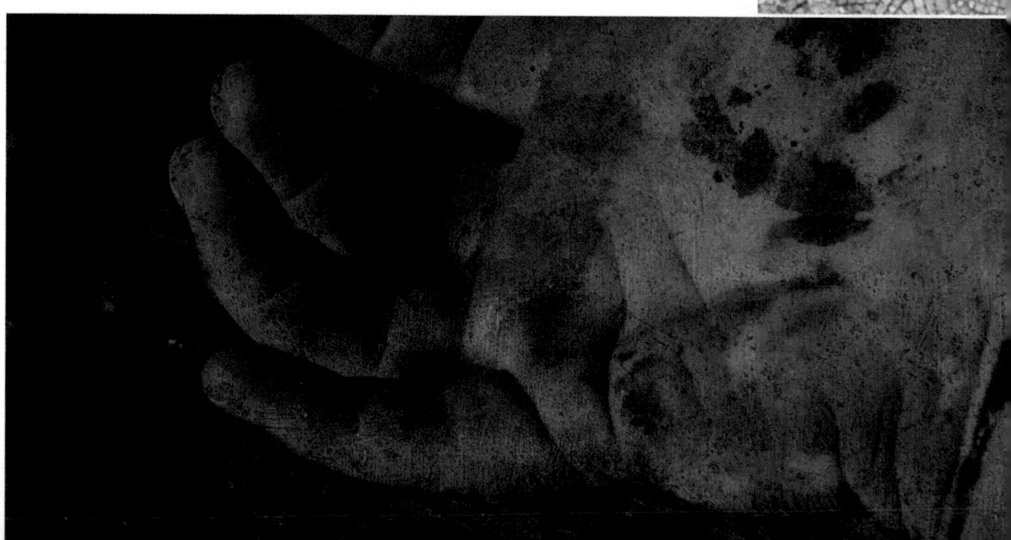

The soldiers made fun of Jesus and brought him some wine. They said, "If you are the king of the Jews, save yourself!"

Luke 23:36-37

WHY THE CRUCIFIXION?

Behold, the lamb of God

Faith invites us to view Christ's ordeal from two perspectives. First, there is the scene described above—the smell of sweat mingled with blood, the darkness that eyewitnesses recount fell over the city, the groans of the suffering men—the bare facts of crucifixion. But behind these grim details is the glorious plan of God.

The crucifixion personalizes Jesus' sacrifice. There, exposed for all to see, is a man who claimed to be God's own Son: naked, beaten, utterly deserted. The robber beside him, suffering his own hellish death, was the only one to offer a kind word. The rest of his supporters stood at a distance, watching (Luke 23:49). Jesus suffered as a human, but he also suffered as the innocent Son of God, made to feel the full weight of God the Father's justice, poured out on a world overflowing with grief and sin—all so humanity could be forgiven.

The crucifixion is the lowest point of the New Testament, the nadir of both the Easter story and of the history of humanity. At the moment of Jesus' death, when he cries to heaven in a pain-wracked voice, asking why he was being forsaken, the Gospels recount that darkness fell over Jerusalem (Mark 15:33–34). Matthew writes of marvels far outside the natural order of this world: the earth shook and the dead rose up and walked about the city (Matthew 27:51–53).

Yet in another sense, the crucifixion is Jesus' greatest hour, his moment of triumph. One of the soldiers standing watch exclaimed that Jesus was surely the Son of God (Matthew 27:54).

At that point, Jesus' followers had only his cryptic promise of resurrection to comfort themselves. As they carried his shattered body to the tomb, the overwhelming finality of his death, which they had all witnessed, oppressed them with crushing grief.

The Thieves

As Jesus suffered on the cross that Friday, a microcosm of the world's reaction to his death unfolded beside him. Two criminals, sentenced to death for their crimes, endured their own prolonged ordeals along with him. The first, embittered by his physical pain and none-too-happy life, hurled sarcastic demands at Jesus: "Aren't you the Messiah? Save yourself and save us!"

It isn't hard to understand such an attitude; the man beside him had been celebrated for raising people from the dead and walking on water. He had even claimed to be God's own Son. And now he seemed no different from the broken, powerless criminal who taunted him.

But the other thief presented an alternative to despair: he clung to his faith against, all odds, in the very darkest hour of adversity. "Don't you fear God?" he asked. Those four words contained his belief. He turned toward Jesus and with reverence asked Jesus to remember him. And with compassion and authority in his voice, Jesus promised him paradise (Luke 23:39–43).

Medical Report: What Happened to Jesus' Body?

Hermatidrosis: Luke recounts that just before Jesus' arrest in the Garden of Gethsemane, his sweat appeared to be like drops of blood (22:44). This medical condition has been observed in cases of extreme psychic stress, when capillaries near the skin's surface rupture and mix with sweat.

Hypovolemic shock: The punishment of scourging, which often preceded crucifixion, frequently resulted in blood loss to the point of shock. It was often accompanied by symptoms of delirium, fainting, vomiting, and in the most extreme cases, death.

Crucifixion: Exhausted from extreme emotional and physical stress, a crucified prisoner would literally gasp for air as his full body weight bore down on his lungs. Incredible thirst, that basic human need, would overcome the body as it desperately tried to compensate for the loss of blood. These agonies might last for hours as the major systems of the body collapsed.

Liturgical churches remember this period when Christ lay in the tomb with the traditional Easter Vigil, considered by the Roman Catholic Church and the Anglican Communion (and some other liturgical faith traditions) as the most important Mass of the church calendar. It is held in the hours of darkness between sunset on Holy Saturday and sunrise on Easter Day.

Holy Saturday is sometimes called Easter Eve. In the Philippines, it is called Black Saturday; in the Czech Republic and Slovakia it is called White Saturday (probably because of the white garments of the newly baptized). On the day that we now call Holy Saturday, Jesus' body was still in the tomb.

In Eastern Orthodoxy this day is also called The Great Sabbath, since it is said on this day Christ "rested" in the tomb, in death, just as the Sabbath is a day of rest in the Jewish tradition.

HOLY SATURDAY

A QUOTE FROM THE BIBLE

JOHN 19:38–42

Joseph from Arimathea was one of Jesus' disciples. He had kept it secret though, because he was afraid of the Jewish leaders. But now he asked Pilate to let him have Jesus' body. Pilate gave him permission, and Joseph took it down from the cross.

Nicodemus also came with about 75 pounds of spices made from myrrh and aloes. This was the same Nicodemus who had visited Jesus one night. The two men wrapped the body in a linen cloth, together with the spices, which was how the Jewish people buried their dead. In the place where Jesus had been nailed to a cross, there was a garden with a tomb that had never been used. The tomb was nearby, and since it was the time to prepare for the Sabbath, they were in a hurry to put Jesus' body there.

The Garden Tomb

Kissing the Stone Of Unction

After being taken down from the cross, Jesus was buried in a tomb donated by a man named Joseph, who lived in the town of Arimathea. Joseph, described in John's Gospel as a disciple of Jesus, was assisted by Nicodemus, who had come to Jesus in secret to learn from him (*see* John 3). Even though Joseph and Nicodemus were members of the first-century religious leadership that so fiercely opposed Jesus' ministry, they were followers of Jesus and, out of love for their teacher, prepared Jesus' body for burial.

Often the graves of the first century were caves carved out of stone. The deceased was laid inside and often, as was the case here, a stone was used to block the opening of the grave. Spices were used to lessen the stench of the body's decay.

Those caring for Jesus' body were in a hurry, for the Sabbath began at sundown on Friday evening. All work was to be completed before this sacred day of rest. Then they all waited—the men who buried Jesus, the women who prepared additional spices for his grave, and the disciples, who seemed unsure of what would happen next.

The women who had come with Jesus from Galilee followed Joseph and watched how Jesus' body was placed in the tomb.

Luke 23:55

Fresco at the wall of Moldovița monastery, Bukovina, Romania

The Resurrection

Christian faith is an Easter faith. The resurrection of Jesus on Easter Sunday is the final seal on his message and his mission. One of Jesus' noted followers, the apostle and theologian Paul (author of many of the New Testament letters) wrote clearly that his own faith would have been empty without the reality of the resurrection. Jesus' resurrection was more than a singular event, and is far more than the end of his story, for its meaning lives on. It represents the beginning of the final resurrection described in the apocalyptic writings in the Bible, and it also represents the beginning of God's ultimate victory over the evil spiritual forces of the world.

The Christian message addresses the plight of humans who choose their own way instead of God's way, a choice that results in both spiritual and physical death. Jesus' death was God's way of dealing with the captivity of humanity to sin and death. Jesus' resurrection is evidence of the redemption that his sacrifice inaugurated—for Christianity promises us that his triumph over death can also be ours.

ction

A QUOTE FROM THE BIBLE

1 CORINTHIANS 15:12-22

If we preach that Christ was raised from death, how can some of you say the dead will not be raised to life? If they won't be raised to life, Christ himself wasn't raised to life. And if Christ wasn't raised to life, our message is worthless, and so is your faith. If the dead won't be raised to life, we have told lies about God by saying he raised Christ to life, when he really did not.

So if the dead won't be raised to life, Christ wasn't raised to life. Unless Christ was raised to life, your faith is useless, and you are still living in your sins. And those people who died after putting their faith in him are completely lost. If our hope in Christ is good only for this life, we are worse off than anyone else.

But Christ has been raised to life! And he makes us certain that others will also be raised to life. Just as we will die because of Adam, we will be raised to life because of Christ. Adam brought death to all of us, and Christ will bring life to all of us.

Theories vs. Literary Witnesses

After Jesus' death on the cross, he was quickly buried before the Sabbath commenced, according to Jewish law. The Sabbath began at sundown on Friday evening and ended at sundown on Saturday evening. Thus, it was not until the first light of Sunday morning that the women who mourned Christ's death were permitted to go to the tomb with the spices that were customarily used to block the stench of the body's decay.

While each of the four Gospels offers details specific to its author's perspective, they all report that these women were the first to find the tomb empty and Jesus gone.

Through the years, many theories have tried to explain why Jesus' tomb might be empty—if he did not indeed rise from the dead. Here are several of the most popular of them, along with the arguments that refute them:

- **Jesus didn't really die on the cross. He merely fainted, then later came to his senses and went on his way.**
  Consider: The soldiers that executed Jesus were professionals, who regularly oversaw the execution of criminals. Would they be that easily fooled?
- **The women simply went to the wrong tomb, one that was empty.**
  Consider: Did everyone go to the wrong tomb? This was not a modern cemetery, with one identical gravesite after another. The Bible states specifically that the women noted the location of the tomb so that they would be able to return (Matthew 27:61; Mark 15:47; Luke 23:55).
- **The disciples stole Jesus' body in order to fake his resurrection.**
  Consider: To prevent this from happening, Pilate ordered soldiers to guard the tomb (Matthew 27:62–66). Even those who reject the reality of the resurrection confirm that Jesus' disciples believed him to be alive.

(Continued on following page)

A QUOTE FROM THE BIBLE

1 PETER 1:3

Praise God, the Father of our Lord Jesus Christ. God is so good, and by raising Jesus from death, he has given us new life and a hope that lives on.

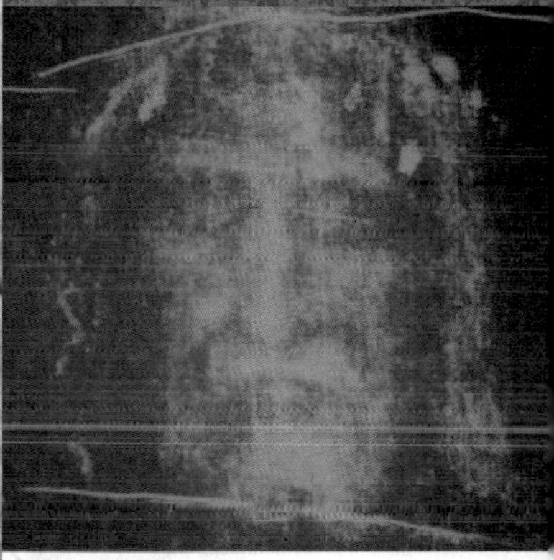

The Shroud of Turin

The Shroud of Turin is a burial cloth on which the image of a crucified man is imprinted. Many people claim this imprint was made when the body of Jesus was wrapped in this shroud, then resurrected through it. The cloth was housed in the cathedral in Turin, Italy, for hundreds of years. Some still believe in the authenticity of the shroud, but even our modern scientific tools cannot verify that claim.

Tapestry detail from the Vatican museum showing the resurrection of Jesus Christ

- **The disciples simply had visions of Jesus after his death—they didn't physically see him. The resurrection "legend" grew as time passed.**
  Consider: In order to accept this, one has to accept that none of the details of the resurrection accounts are true. Yet the Gospel accounts have historical credibility that can be dated to years, not centuries, after Jesus lived.

None of these theories do an effective job of refuting the historical accounts of the resurrection as reported by the literary witnesses. While these accounts may not be completely verifiable by today's scientific and forensic terms, they do bear strong credibility as historical evidence. Jesus' post-resurrection appearances, as cited in all four Gospels, are some of the most compelling evidence for the validity of the resurrection.

Here is what literary witnesses reported concerning Jesus' resurrection, according to the Gospel accounts, and according to the apostle Paul:

1

Jesus was put to death by crucifixion.

2

He was buried in the tomb of a man named Joseph, from Arimathea.

3

The tomb was found empty within days of his burial.

4

After his resurrection, Jesus appeared to a variety of people. In only one of those cases, involving the apostle Paul, was the appearance clearly described as a vision.

5

The disciples, who had been left doubting and somewhat defeated by the crucifixion of Christ, were quickly transformed by his resurrection, and went on to organize their efforts to spread Jesus' message to the entire world.

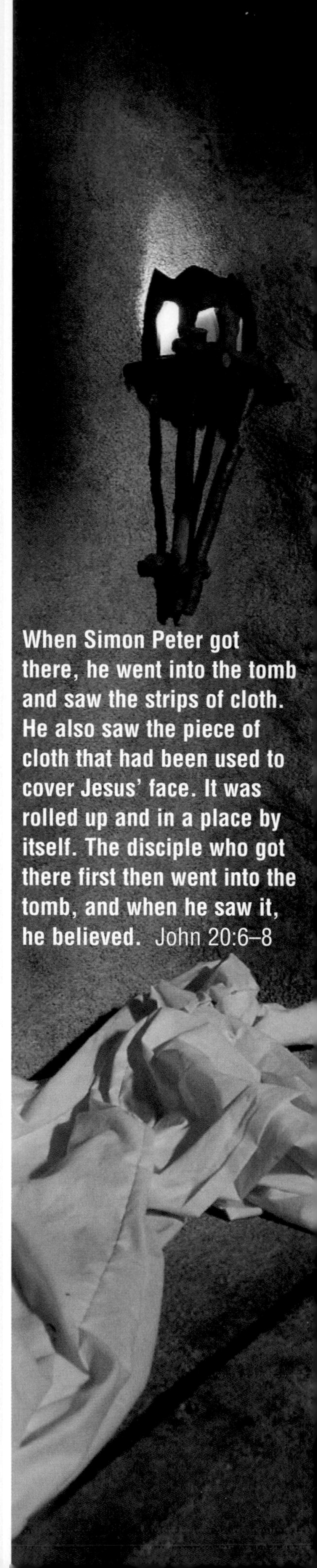

When Simon Peter got there, he went into the tomb and saw the strips of cloth. He also saw the piece of cloth that had been used to cover Jesus' face. It was rolled up and in a place by itself. The disciple who got there first then went into the tomb, and when he saw it, he believed. John 20:6–8

TRADITION & TRUTH

WHEN IS EASTER?

THE BIBLE DOES NOT TELL US THE DATE OF JESUS' RESURRECTION, BUT IT DOES SAY THESE EVENTS HAPPENED DURING THE WEEK OF THE JEWISH PASSOVER.

TODAY, EASTER IS A MOVABLE FEAST ON THE CHRISTIAN CALENDAR, AS IS PASSOVER ON THE JEWISH CALENDAR. IT IS CELEBRATED AROUND THE SAME TIME EACH YEAR, IN THE SEASON OF SPRING, AS AN OPPORTUNITY TO REMEMBER THE SIGNIFICANT EVENTS OF THE PAST.

FOLLOWING A DECREE BY THE THIRD-CENTURY COUNCIL OF NICEA, EASTER WAS TO BE CELEBRATED ON A SINGLE SUNDAY DURING THE SPRING. HOWEVER, EVEN THEN THERE WAS DISAGREEMENT ABOUT WHETHER TO RELY ON THE LUNAR CALENDAR (WHICH IS BASED ON THE PHASES OF THE MOON) OR THE SOLAR CALENDAR (WHICH IS BASED ON THE EARTH'S REVOLUTION AROUND THE SUN) TO DETERMINE THE EXACT DATE OF EASTER. A COMPROMISE WAS MADE LATER THAT ALLOWED ADVOCATES OF EACH CALENDAR TO BE SATISFIED: EASTER WOULD BE THE FIRST SUNDAY AFTER THE FIRST FULL MOON OF THE SPRING EQUINOX.

TODAY, THE CHRISTIAN WORLD CONTINUES TO USE TWO SYSTEMS TO DETERMINE THE DATE OF EASTER AND OTHER HOLIDAYS. THE WESTERN TRADITION, OBSERVED BY CATHOLICS AND PROTESTANTS, IS BASED ON THE SOLAR CALENDAR INSTITUTED BY POPE GREGORY IN 1582. UNDER THIS GREGORIAN CALENDAR, EASTER IS STILL THE FIRST SUNDAY AFTER THE FIRST FULL MOON OF SPRING.

HOWEVER, THE EASTERN OR ORTHODOX TRADITION STILL RELIES ON THE LUNAR-BASED JULIAN CALENDAR, SO NAMED BECAUSE IT WAS INTRODUCED BY JULIUS CAESAR IN 46 BC. AFTER MANY CENTURIES, THIS LUNAR CALENDAR HAS NOW DIVERGED FROM THE GREGORIAN SOLAR CALENDAR BY MORE THAN 13 DAYS. SINCE THE 28-DAY CYCLE OF THE MOON PLAYS A ROLE IN BOTH CALENDARS, THE DATE OF EASTER SOMETIMES IS THE SAME UNDER BOTH SYSTEMS. YET AT OTHER TIMES THE DATES OF THE OBSERVANCE MAY DIFFER BY AS MUCH AS FIVE WEEKS.

A QUOTE FROM THE BIBLE

PHILIPPIANS 3:7-11

But Christ has shown me that what I once thought was valuable is worthless. Nothing is as wonderful as knowing Christ Jesus my Lord. I have given up everything else and count it all as garbage. All I want is Christ and to know that I belong to him. I could not make myself acceptable to God by obeying the Law of Moses. God accepted me simply because of my faith in Christ. All I want is to know Christ and the power that raised him to life. I want to suffer and die as he did, so that somehow I also may be raised to life.

POST-RESURRECTION APPEARANCES

Jesus' resurrection is recorded in numerous places in the Bible and was reported by many eyewitnesses. Paul records in 1 Corinthians 15:1–11 the longest list of post-resurrection appearances of Jesus.

MY FRIENDS, I WANT YOU TO REMEMBER THE MESSAGE I PREACHED AND THAT YOU BELIEVED AND TRUSTED. YOU WILL BE SAVED BY THIS MESSAGE, IF YOU HOLD FIRMLY TO IT. BUT IF YOU DON'T, YOUR FAITH WAS ALL FOR NOTHING.

I TOLD YOU THE MOST IMPORTANT PART OF THE MESSAGE EXACTLY AS IT WAS TOLD TO ME. THAT PART IS:

CHRIST DIED FOR OUR SINS,
AS THE SCRIPTURES SAY.
HE WAS BURIED,
AND THREE DAYS LATER
HE WAS RAISED TO LIFE,
AS THE SCRIPTURES SAY.
CHRIST APPEARED TO PETER,THEN TO THE TWELVE.
AFTER THIS, HE APPEARED
TO MORE THAN FIVE HUNDRED
OTHER FOLLOWERS.
MOST OF THEM ARE STILL ALIVE,
BUT SOME HAVE DIED.
HE ALSO APPEARED TO JAMES,
AND THEN TO ALL
OF THE APOSTLES.

Christ Appeared.

FINALLY, HE APPEARED TO ME, EVEN THOUGH I AM LIKE SOMEONE WHO WAS BORN AT THE WRONG TIME. I AM THE LEAST IMPORTANT OF ALL THE APOSTLES. IN FACT, I CAUSED SO MUCH TROUBLE FOR GOD'S CHURCH THAT I DON'T EVEN DESERVE TO BE CALLED AN APOSTLE. BUT GOD TREATED ME WITH UNDESERVED GRACE! HE MADE ME WHAT I AM, AND HIS GRACE WASN'T WASTED. I WORKED MUCH HARDER THAN ANY OF THE OTHER APOSTLES, ALTHOUGH IT WAS REALLY GOD'S GRACE AT WORK AND NOT ME. BUT IT DOESN'T MATTER IF I PREACHED OR IF THEY PREACHED. ALL OF YOU BELIEVED THE MESSAGE JUST THE SAME.

BELOW ARE MANY OF THE OTHER NEW TESTAMENT STORIES OF JESUS' POST-RESURRECTION APPEARANCES:

MARY SEES JESUS

Matthew 28:9–10; Mark 16:9; John 20:14–17

JESUS APPEARS TO HIS DISCIPLES IN A LOCKED ROOM

John 20:19–29

JESUS WALKS WITH TWO FOLLOWERS TO EMMAUS

Luke 24:13–32

SEVEN DISCIPLES SEE JESUS ALONG THE SHORE OF LAKE TIBERIAS

John 21:1–14

JESUS GIVES FINAL INSTRUCTIONS TO HIS ELEVEN DISCIPLES

Matthew 28:16–20

JESUS APPEARS TO 500 PEOPLE AT ONCE

1 Corinthians 15:6

JAMES, JESUS' BROTHER, SEES JESUS

1 Corinthians 15:7

THE DISCIPLES SEE JESUS ASCEND TO HEAVEN

Luke 24:50–51; Acts 1:9–11

TRADITION & TRUTH

EASTER LILIES

MANY CHURCHES FILL THEIR SANCTUARIES WITH WHITE LILIES AT EASTER. THIS TRADITION STEMS FROM SEVERAL SOURCES, INCLUDING A LEGEND IN THE EARLY CHURCH THAT LILIES SPRANG UP IN THE GARDEN OF GETHSEMANE ON THE SPOTS WHERE CHRIST'S SWEAT AND TEARS FELL DURING HIS FINAL HOURS BEFORE HE WAS BETRAYED BY JUDAS. OTHER TRADITIONS POINT TO THE LILY AS A FLOWER THAT PROCLAIMS HOPE, BEAUTY, AND NURTURE.

IN ROMAN MYTHOLOGY, LILIES APPEAR IN THE STORY OF JUNO, THE QUEEN OF THE GODS, WHO SPILLS MILK WHILE NURSING HER SON, HERCULES. ACCORDING TO THIS TALE, PART OF THE MILK REMAINED IN THE SKY AND FORMED WHAT WE CALL TODAY THE MILKY WAY, AND THE REST FELL TO EARTH AND SPRANG TO LIFE AS LILIES. PURE WHITE LILIES HAVE OFTEN BEEN USED IN PAINTINGS OF MARY TO REPRESENT CHRIST'S VIRGIN BIRTH.

The Ascension

Luke's Gospel ends with a description of Jesus' ascent to heaven. This ascent is described in more detail in Acts 1:1–11, a book also written by Luke. The Acts account reveals that Jesus ascended from the Mount of Olives, east of Jerusalem, near a town called Bethany.

After his resurrection, Jesus spent time with his followers, instructing them how to carry on his work. He also made them promises, including the promise that the Holy Spirit would come upon them and give them power.

Jesus' ascension changed the relationship between God and humanity. The work he came to do had been completed, allowing each of us to connect with God in a new way. Before Christ's mission, we could only hope for a future reconciliation with God; now we can base our hope on the reality of Jesus' sacrifice. While the Spirit of God has existed since before time, the work of Jesus inaugurated a new kind of relationship, in which God's Spirit lives inside his reconciled people, teaching and leading them in the ways of the kingdom.

Jesus said to them, "You don't need to know the time of those events that only the Father controls. But the Holy Spirit will come upon you and give you power. Then you will tell everyone about me in Jerusalem, in all Judea, in Samaria, and everywhere in the world." After Jesus had said this and while they were watching, he was taken up into a cloud. They could not see him, but as he went up, they kept looking up into the sky.

Acts 1:7–10

Saint Isaak Cathedral, interior of the main dome.

TRADITION & TRUTH

BUNNIES, BASKETS, AND EGGS

THE MODERN HOLIDAY TRADITION OF THE EASTER BUNNY DEMONSTRATES THE ENDURING POWER OF OLD FOLKLORES AND MYTHOLOGIES. SINCE ANCIENT PRE-CHRISTIAN TIMES, RABBITS HAVE BEEN A SYMBOL OF FERTILITY. THE EASTER BUNNY IS THE RESULT OF MERGING THE PAGAN CELEBRATION OF SPRING-TIME RENEWAL FOLLOWING THE BARREN WINTER WITH THE CHRISTIAN TRADITION OF CELEBRATING CHRIST'S RESURRECTION ON EASTER. ACTUALLY, EARLY CHRISTIAN LEADERS PROBABLY ALLOWED PAGAN CUSTOMS AND FEASTS TO BE INCORPORATED INTO CHRISTIAN CELEBRATIONS IN ORDER TO WIN OVER CONVERTS TO THE FAITH. DURING THE SECOND CENTURY, A SPRING FESTIVAL CELEBRATED IN MUCH OF THE ROMAN EMPIRE HONORED THE SAXON GODDESS EASTRE, WHOSE SACRED ANIMAL WAS A RABBIT! THE TRADITION CHANGED OVER THE CENTURIES, AND THE GERMANS ARE CREDITED WITH STARTING THE TRADITION OF SURPRISING THEIR CHILDREN WITH COLORED EGGS IN NESTS DELIVERED ON EASTER MORNING BY A KINDLY RABBIT. GERMAN IMMIGRANTS BROUGHT THE TRADITION TO THE UNITED STATES, WHERE TODAY THE EASTER BUNNY HERALDS THE ARRIVAL OF SPRING AND A HOLIDAY THAT COMMEMORATES CHRIST'S REBIRTH FROM THE GRAVE WITH BASKETS FULL OF CANDY-COLORED EGGS.

EGGS ARE AN OBVIOUS SYMBOL FOR FERTILITY, AND EVEN THE ANCIENT GREEKS AND ROMANS DECORATED THEM TO CELEBRATE REBIRTH AND ABUNDANCE IN SPRINGTIME. THERE IS SOME CONTROVERSY SURROUNDING THE ADOPTION OF THESE TRADITIONS, DUE TO THEIR PAGAN ORIGINS. HOWEVER, MOST CHRISTIANS CONSIDER THEM A HARMLESS WAY TO CELEBRATE CHRIST'S GLORIOUS TRIUMPH OVER DEATH AND THE POWER OF DIVINE SALVATION TO BRING REBIRTH TO ALL GOD'S CREATION.

The Coming of The Holy Spirit

[JESUS SAID] I AM SAYING THIS TO YOU NOW, SO THAT WHEN THE TIME COMES, YOU WILL REMEMBER WHAT I HAVE SAID.

I WAS WITH YOU AT THE FIRST, AND SO I DIDN'T TELL YOU THESE THINGS. BUT NOW I AM GOING BACK TO THE FATHER WHO SENT ME, AND NONE OF YOU ASKS ME WHERE I AM GOING. YOU ARE VERY SAD FROM HEARING ALL OF THIS. BUT I TELL YOU I AM GOING TO DO WHAT IS BEST FOR YOU. THIS IS WHY I AM GOING AWAY. THE HOLY SPIRIT CANNOT COME TO HELP YOU UNTIL I LEAVE. BUT AFTER I AM GONE, I WILL SEND THE SPIRIT TO YOU.

THE SPIRIT WILL COME AND SHOW THE PEOPLE OF THIS WORLD THE TRUTH ABOUT SIN AND GOD'S JUSTICE AND THE JUDGMENT . . . . I HAVE MUCH MORE TO SAY TO YOU, BUT RIGHT NOW IT WOULD BE MORE THAN YOU COULD UNDERSTAND. THE SPIRIT SHOWS WHAT IS TRUE AND WILL COME AND GUIDE YOU INTO THE FULL TRUTH. THE SPIRIT DOESN'T SPEAK ON HIS OWN. HE WILL TELL YOU ONLY WHAT HE HAS HEARD FROM ME, AND HE WILL LET YOU KNOW WHAT IS GOING TO HAPPEN. THE SPIRIT WILL BRING GLORY TO ME BY TAKING MY MESSAGE AND TELLING IT TO YOU.

JOHN 16:4–14

Pentecost.
Oil on canvas.
Restout, Jean (1663–1702)
Location: Louvre, Paris, France

EPILOGUE

The story of Jesus of Nazareth does not end with his death, resurrection, and ascension to heaven. His contemporaries left their accounts of his life, his sayings, his miraculous deeds and his challenging message so that they would resound throughout history. And they have. But Jesus, as Son of God, offers us more than simply an inspiring life story or an example to be followed: he promised his followers access to God's ongoing presence, as alive in our time as in his time, present in us and through us, even beyond death.

Jesus promised that he would make his home in those who show their love for him by obeying his teachings (John 14:23–27). One foundation of those teachings is his message that we should live our faith authentically, not as it is defined by religious rules or traditions, and always informed by a love of God and a love for others, even for those who may not return that love. In Jesus' final prayers before the arrest that led to his trials and crucifixion, he prayed not only for the disciples who were present that night, but also for the disciples who would follow in their footsteps generations later (John 17:6–24):

> *You have given me some followers from this world, and I have shown them what you are like. They were yours, but you gave them to me, and they have obeyed you. . . . I have given myself completely for their sake, so they may belong completely to the truth.*
>
> *I am not praying just for these followers. I am also praying for everyone else who will have faith because of what my followers will say about me. I want all of them to be one with each other, just as I am one with you and you are one with me. I also want them to be one with us. Then the people of this world will believe that you sent me* (John 17: 6, 19–21).

Jesus answered: "Love the Lord your God with all your heart, soul, and mind. This is the first and most important commandment." The second most important commandment is like this one. And it is, "Love others as much as you love yourself." All the Law of Moses and the Books of the Prophets are based on these two commandments.

Matthew 22:38-40

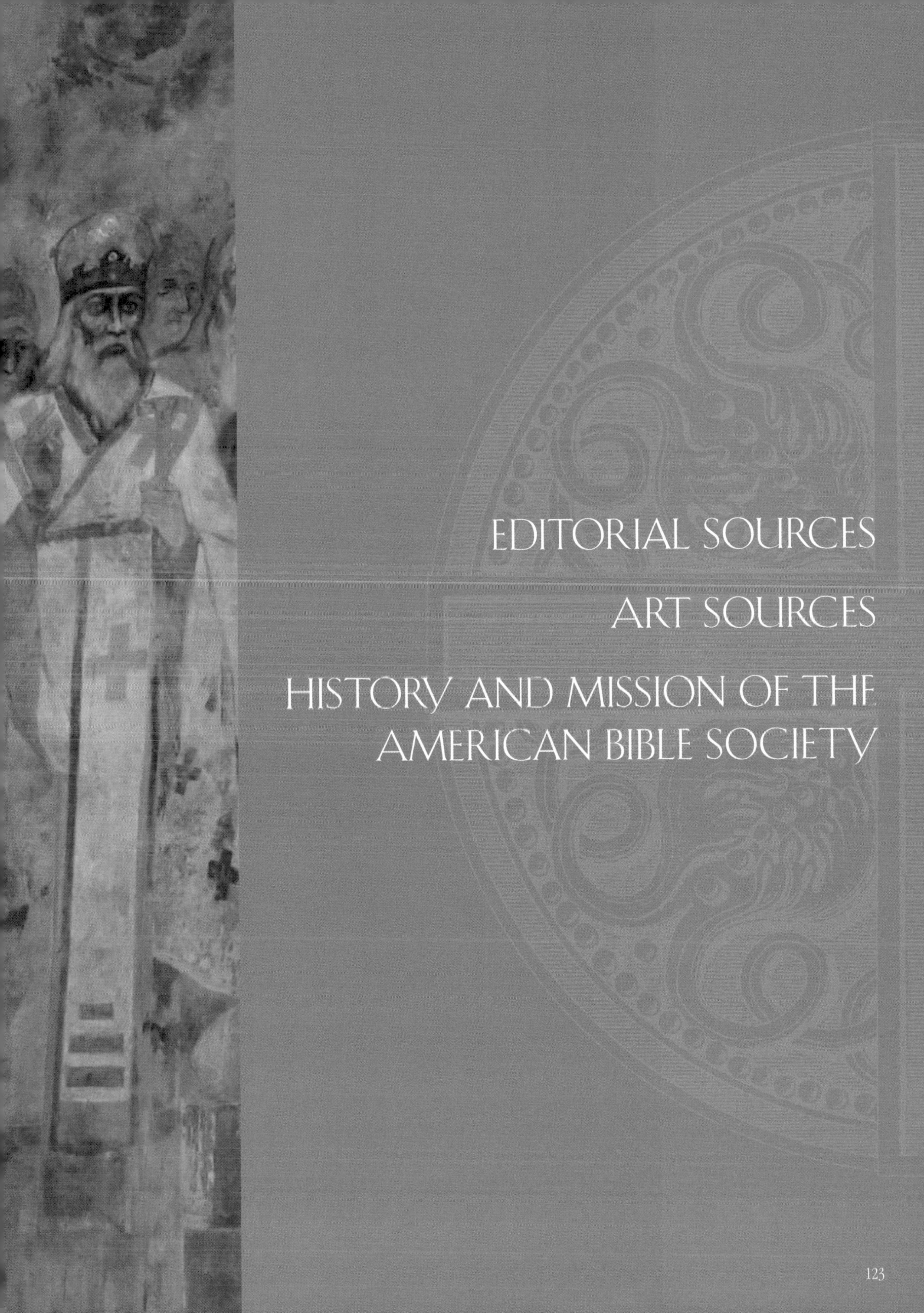

EDITORIAL SOURCES

ART SOURCES

HISTORY AND MISSION OF THE AMERICAN BIBLE SOCIETY

The Life of Christ is not intended to be a definitive source of information; rather, it was written to invite you to explore for yourself what the life and work of Jesus Christ reveals about God and His relationship with humanity. As we compiled our research, we took great care to question and verify. Now, we offer you the opportunity to research and verify our findings as well, and we invite you to further explore the life and teachings of Jesus Christ for yourself.

EDITORIAL SOURCES

The following resources were used to develop the material in this book.

1. Books written on specific topics
2. Bible dictionaries or encyclopedias with entries for people, places, and events
3. Commentaries that explore the Bible text by sections of verses
4. Magazine articles
5. Credible online sources

ARTICLES

- Brown, Farrell. April 1, 2004. "Why Does Easter's Date Wander?" *Christianity Today.*
- Lacey, Marc. April 1, 2007. "U.S. Churches Go 'Green' for Palm Sunday." *The New York Times.*
- Miller, Dave. 2004. "Did Jesus Sweat Blood?" *Apologetics Press.*
  Full text: http://www.apologeticspress.org/articles/2223.
- Milwitzky, William. "Antipas" (Herod Antipas). *Jewish Encyclopedia.* Funk & Wagnalls.
- Seiglie, Mario. November/December 1999. "Removing the Myths of Christ's Childhood."
  The Good News: A Magazine of Understanding.

BOOKS

- Elwell, Walter A. and Philip W. Comfort, eds. 2001. *Tyndale Bible Dictionary.* Tyndale House Publishers.
- Hock, Ronald F. 1996. *The Infancy Gospels of James and Thomas: with Introduction, Notes, and Original Text Featuring the New Scholars Version Translation.* Polebridge Press.
- Knight, George W. and Rayburn W. Ray, eds. 2005. *The Illustrated Everyday Bible Companion.* Barbour
- Koester, Helmut. 1990. *Ancient Christian Gospels: Their History and Development.* Trinity Press International.
- Strauss, Mark L. 2007. *Four Portraits, One Jesus.* Zondervan.
- Zugibe, F. T. 1988. *The Cross and the Shroud: a Medical Inquiry Into the Crucifixion.* Penguin Press.

ONLINE SOURCES

about.com
americancatholic.org
answers.com
apologeticspress.org
biblestudy.org
britannica.com
catholicculture.org
christmasspirit.wordpress.com
dpsw.org
en.wikipedia.org
explorefaith.org
gnmagazine.org
kencollins.com
newadvent.org
omnigraphics.com
pravmir.com
theholidayspot.com
wf-f.org

ART SOURCES

Art Resource

Magi Before King Herod (antebaptistry).
1343–54, Byzantine mosaic.
Location: S. Marco, Venice, Italy
Photo Credit: Cameraphoto / Art Resource, NY

Rembrandt Harmensz van Rijn (1606–1669) (attributed to).
Head of Christ, 17th Century. Oil on panel, enlarged on all sides;
9 ¹/₄ x 7 ⁷/₈ inches (24.8 x 20 cm). John G. Johnson Collection, 1917.
Location: Philadelphia Museum of Art, Philadelphia, Pennsylvania, U.S.A.
Photo Credit: The Philadelphia Museum of Art / Art Resource, NY

Beck, Walter (1864–1954)
Christ Before Pilate. Undated. Pastel. 48 x 32 in. (121.9 x 81.3 cm).
Location: Smithsonian American Art Museum, Washington, DC, U.S.A.
Photo Credit: Smithsonian American Art Museum, Washington, DC / Art Resource, NY

Cavallini, Pietro (c.1250–1330)
Adoration of the Magi. Mosaic.
Location: S. Maria in Trastevere, Rome, Italy
Photo Credit: Scala / Art Resource, NY

Christ Crowned with Thorns. Wood.
Filipino School (20th Century)
Private Collection
Photo: Boltin Picture Library/The Bridgeman Art Library
Nationality/copyright status: Filipino/copyright unknown

Christ Heals a Blind Man. Relief (3rd CE) on an early Christian sarcophagus
from Mezzocamino, Via Ostiense, Rome. Cat. 41.
Location: Museo Nazionale Romano (Terme di Diocleziano),
Museo Nazionale Romano, Rome, Italy
Photo Credit: Erich Lessing / Art Resource, NY

The Miracle of Christ Turning the Water Into Wine At the Marriage at Cana.
Early Christian mosaic. 6th CE.
Location: S. Apollinare Nuovo, Ravenna, Italy
Photo Credit: Scala / Art Resource, NY

Tissot, James Jacques Joseph (1836–1902)
Jesus Casting Devils Out of a Kneeling Man, c1890.
Location: Ann Ronan Picture Library, London, Great Britain
Photo Credit: HIP / Art Resource, NY

Ciseri, Antonio (1821–1891)
Ecce Homo. 1891. Oil on canvas, 292 x 380 cm.
Location: Galleria d'Arte Moderna, Florence, Italy
Photo Credit: Alinari / Art Resource, NY

Heavenly Jerusalem. Early Christian mosaic. 5th CE.
Location: S. Maria Maggiore, Rome, Italy
Photo Credit: Nimatallah / Art Resource, NY

Batoni, Pompeo (1708–1787)
The Return of the Prodigal Son (Luke 15,11–32).
Oil on canvas (1773), 173 x 122 cm. Inv. 148.
Location: Kunsthistorisches Museum, Vienna, Austria
Photo Credit: Erich Lessing / Art Resource, NY

Jesus praying. Detail from *The Prayer in the Garden of Gethsemane*.
Byzantine fresco. 14th CE.
Location: Monastery Church, Ohrid, Macedonia
Photo Credit: Erich Lessing / Art Resource, NY

Sodoma, Giovanni Antonio Bazzi, called Il (1477–1549)
Christ Presented to the People (Ecce Homo). Oil on canvas, 23 ⁵/₈ x 23 ¹/₄ in.
(60 x 59.1 cm). Gift of Asbjorn R. Lunde, in memory of his parents,
Karl and Elisa Lunde, 1996 (1996.261).
Location: The Metropolitan Museum of Art, New York, NY, U.S.A.
Photo Credit: Image copyright ©The Metropolitan Museum of Art / Art Resource, NY

Le Brun, Charles (1619–1690)
Christ's Entry into Jerusalem. Oil on canvas. 153 x 214 cm.
INVD62-1-1. Photo: René-Gabriel Ojéda.
Location: Musee d'Art et d'Industrie, Saint-Etienne, France
Photo Credit: Réunion des Musées Nationaux / Art Resource, NY

Liebermann, Max (1847–1935)
The 12-Year-Old Jesus in the Temple. 1879. Oil on canvas,
149.6 x 130.8 cm. Inv.: 5424.
Location: Hamburger Kunsthalle, Hamburg, Germany
Photo Credit: Bildarchiv Preussischer Kulturbesitz / Art Resource, NY

Luca di Tomme (1330–after 1389)
Resurrection of Lazarus.
Location: Pinacoteca, Vatican Museums, Vatican State
Photo Credit: Scala / Art Resource, NY

Restout, Jean (1663–1702)
Pentecost. Oil on canvas.
Photo: Moulonguet/Ojeda.
Location: Louvre, Paris, France
Photo Credit: Réunion des Musées Nationaux / Art Resource, NY

Chiari, Giuseppe (1654–1727)
The Sermon on the Mount. Ca. 1680. Oil on canvas, 100 x 138 cm.
Photo: Roman Beniaminson.
Location: State Museum of Fine Art, Sebastopol, Ukraine
Photo Credit: Bildarchiv Preussischer Kulturbesitz / Art Resource, NY

Getty Images

RL000037 (RF) *Mosaic Deisis Detail*
Collection: Photodisc Green
Photographer: Andrew Ward/Life File

Dover Electronic Clip Art

Bible Illustrations

FotoSearch

www.fotosearch.com
Christian Faith Vol. 1, Christian Faith Vol. 2, Christian Faith Vol. 3

Dreamstime

www.dreamstime.com

All other images:

iStock Photo, www.istockphoto.com

History and Mission of the American Bible Society

Since the establishment of the American Bible Society in 1816, its history has been closely intertwined with the history of the nation whose name it bears. In fact, the Society's early leadership reads like a *Who's Who* of patriots and other American movers and shakers. Its first president was Elias Boudinot, formerly the President of the Continental Congress. John Jay, John Quincy Adams, DeWitt Clinton, and chronicler of the new nation James Fenimore Cooper also played significant roles in the Society's history, as would Rutherford B. Hayes and Benjamin Harrison in later generations.

From the beginning, the Bible Society's mission has been to respond to the spiritual needs of a fast-growing, diverse population in a rapidly expanding nation. From the new frontier beyond the Appalachian Mountains, missionaries sent back dire reports of towns that did not have a single copy of the Bible to share among its citizens. State and local Bible Societies did not have the resources, network, or capabilities to fill this growing need: a national organization was called for. The ABS committed itself to organizational and technological innovations to meet the demand. No longer subject to British restrictions, the ABS could set up its own printing plants, develop better qualities of paper and ink, and establish a network of colporteurs to get the Bibles to the people who needed them.

Reaching out to diverse audiences has always been at the heart of ABS's mission. Scriptures were made available to Native peoples in their own languages—in Delaware in 1818, followed soon by Mohawk, Seneca, Ojibwa, Cherokee, and others. French and Spanish Bibles were published for the Louisiana Territory, Florida, and the Southwest. By the 1890s the ABS was printing or distributing Scriptures in German, Portuguese, Chinese, Italian, Russian, Danish, Polish, Hungarian, Czech, and other languages to meet the spiritual needs of an increasing immigrant population. In 1836, 75 years before the first Braille Bibles were produced, the ABS was providing Scriptures to the blind in "raised letter" editions.

Responding to the need for Bibles in the languages and formats that speak most deeply to people's hearts continues to be a priority of the ABS. Through its partnerships with other national Bible Societies, the ABS can provide some portion of Scripture in almost any language that has a written form. It has also been able to provide Braille Scriptures for the blind, as well as recorded Scriptures for the visually impaired, dyslexic, and people who have not yet learned to read.

The Bible Society's founders and their successors have always understood the Bible as a text that can speak to people's deepest needs in times of crisis. During the War of 1812, the ABS distributed its first Scriptures to the military when it provided New Testaments to the crew of the USS *John Adams*. During the Civil War, the ABS provided Testaments to both northern and southern forces, and it has continued to provide Bibles and Testaments to the U.S. military forces during every subsequent war, conflict, and operation. During the painful post-Reconstruction era, when Jim Crow laws prevailed in many parts of the nation, the ABS was able to provide Scriptures to African Americans through its partnership with the Agency Among Colored People of the South and through the historic Black churches.

This faith that the Word of God speaks in special ways during times of crisis continues to inform the ABS mission. In recent years the Bible Society has produced Scripture booklets addressing the needs of people with HIV/AIDS and of those experiencing profound loss due to acts of terrorism and natural disasters.

Translation and scholarship are key components in the Bible Society's mission of communicating the Word of God faithfully and powerfully. In the mid-20th century, the ABS, in partnership with the United Bible Societies, developed innovative theories and practices of translation. First, they insisted that all the Bible translations they sponsored were to be created exclusively by native speakers, with biblical and linguistic experts serving only as translation consultants to provide technical support and guidance. From the lively and heartfelt translations that resulted, Bible Society scholars were able to see the power of translations that were rendered not on a word-for-word basis, but on a meaning-for-meaning basis that respected the natural rhythms and idioms of the target languages. This practice of "functional equivalence" translation reinvigorated the practice of translating the Bible into English and is partly responsible for the explosion of new translations of the Bible that have been issued in the past thirty years. These include the Bible Society's own *Good News Translation* and *Contemporary English Version*, but also the *New International Version*, *New Revised Standard Version*, *Today's Century Version*, *New Living Translation*, and *The Message*.

As an organization dedicated to preparing well-researched, faithful translations, the ABS has necessarily committed itself to the pursuit of scholarly excellence. In cooperation with the United Bible Societies, the ABS has helped develop and publish authoritative Greek and Hebrew texts, handbooks on the different books of the Bible, dictionaries, and other technical aids. To make sure that all relevant disciplines are explored, the Bible Society's Nida Institute for Biblical Scholarship convenes symposia and conferences that invite both academic specialists and practicing translators to gather and exchange ideas that will assist translators in communicating the Bible's message to new audiences. For churches and readers seeking a deeper understanding of the Bible and its background, the ABS has developed study Bibles, multimedia video translations with DVD extras, Scriptures in special formats, and website resources.

For almost two centuries the American Bible Society has maintained its commitment to innovation and excellence. While the challenges it has faced over the years have changed, the Society's mission has remained constant—*to make the Bible available to every person in a language and format each can understand and afford, so all people may experience its life-changing message.*

To find out more about the American Bible Society please go to **www.bibles.com** or **www.877thebible.com**.

the LIFE OF CHRIST